Redeeming Dementia

SPIRITUALITY, THEOLOGY, AND SCIENCE

✳ ✳ ✳

Dorothy Linthicum and Janice Hicks

CHURCH
PUBLISHING
INCORPORATED

Church Publishing
19 East 34th Street
New York, NY 10016
www.churchpublishing.org

Illustrations by Alice Thornburgh

Cover design by Jennifer Kopec, 2Pug Design

Typeset by PerfecType, Nashville, Tennessee

Library of Congress Cataloging-in-Publication Data

A record of this book is available from the Library of Congress.

ISBN-13: 978-1-64065-056-5 (pbk.)
ISBN-13: 978-1-64065-057-2 (ebook)

Printed in Canada

Contents

Acknowledgments

This book is inspired by the love, values, and persistence throughout life's struggles taught to each of us by our parents who had dementia: Nan and Norval Spleth and Helen Hicks. The strength of their faith ultimately deepened our relationship with God and reaffirmed our understanding of the redemptive power of God's grace and love for all people, including those with dementia.

Dorothy's husband, Tom Linthicum, and her brother Tom Spleth, walked with her throughout the years of caregiving and the writing of this book. Janice thanks her brothers, Rick and Jeff Hicks, and all the family for their steadfast support, along with the wonderful people of St. Margaret's Episcopal Church for their support over the years.

Colleagues at Virginia Theological Seminary supported the creation of this book in many ways. Lisa Kimball played an important role in Dorothy's understanding of aging and dementia by supporting her work in this area and giving her time and teaching opportunities to test new ideas. Anne Karoly allowed Dorothy to share the ups and downs of living with her mother, Marilyn, who had dementia. Janice would like to thank Katherine Sonderegger, who served as advisor on a senior thesis on part of this work and was a great source of inspiration. She also gratefully acknowledges Day Smith Pritchartt and the Episcopal Evangelism Society for grant support during the research phase of this work, as well as the input of many clergy and dementia professionals in the United Kingdom and in the United States, particularly the greater Washington, DC, area.

Finally, we would like to thank Sharon Pearson and Church Publishing for the opportunity and the tremendous support during the writing of this book.

Preface

Our background in spirituality, science, and theology, as well as the time we spent with people who have dementia, has brought us to a new understanding of dementia and God's powerful, redeeming love. Our journey began in a classroom at Virginia Theological Seminary, but our experiences long preceded that encounter.

✳ ✳ ✳

At the Abundant Living Conference sponsored by the Episcopal Diocese of Texas several years ago, James S. Goodwin talked about the demonizing of dementia. He concluded by suggesting dementia was really just a learning disability. My reaction was visceral. I felt that he trivialized the final years of my mother's and father's lives, both having had Alzheimer's disease—two words that Goodwin, a medical doctor who has worked with hundreds of people with Alzheimer's, said are overused and fear-inducing. Perhaps, however, the reason his words stung so much was my feeling that the chunk of my life I had spent as a caregiver had also been undervalued. I left that session reeling with uncertainty and anger. To my mind, a progressive brain disease is very different than a learning disability.

The first person I bumped into after Goodwin's talk was Robert Atchley, a man of wisdom whose books and articles I had read and whom I had met at the conference and already learned to trust. I had hoped for a pastoral response. What I got was a curt observation that obviously Goodwin spoke a truth that I needed to examine. In so many words, I was told to "deal with it." And that is what I did for the next year. Goodwin's truth, which I am still untangling from my narrow experience of pain and loss, forced me to look more closely into the science, theology, and spirituality of dementia to better understand it. Goodwin nudged me into a time of discovery that led to the publication of this book. Looking back, I see that God acts in our lives if we only open the eyes of our hearts to watch it happen.—*Dorothy*

✳ ✳ ✳

Facing Our Fears

Dorothy has found that the one variable that almost always comes up when she gives a presentation or leads a workshop about spirituality and aging is people's fear of dementia. It is the elephant in the room. People fear the loss of control it inevitably brings and the loss of relationships with those they love. They begin looking for signs of it in their own actions and in those of the ones they care about. Along with a sense of dread comes a feeling that dementia is the result of a moral failure or that the person is somehow to blame. It is something few want to talk about, and it continues to be surrounded by secrecy and misinformation. The social stigma about mental health in general keeps people from reaching out to one another when they most need to.

In her book *Finding Magic*,[1] Sally Quinn, former reporter at the *Washington Post*, discusses her marriage to Ben Bradlee, former executive director of the *Post*, and living with his dementia in the years before his death in 2014. She describes how colleagues and family members protected Bradlee, but never openly talked with him about his dementia. In 2012, several years into his disease, Quinn began telling close associates that Bradlee had dementia. "It was done. We were heading into a new life, a life I was dreading, and yet a life that would be fulfilling in a way that I never could have imagined."[2]

When others refer to their fear of dementia, we have learned that confronting the reality of dementia head-on is the best way to deal with it. The telling of our stories is the best antidote to get some perspective and ease fears.

✳ ✳ ✳

An unnerving and recurring experience happened at night during my visits home to see my mom, who had dementia, and my dad. Mom, unable to sleep and troubled with a longing to "go home," would roam through the house, stopping at every door in silence, watching. I would lie motionless in my childhood room, hoping she wouldn't venture in. I didn't know this person whose memories of our life together seemed to be erased. So I lay in motionless silence and dread.

I recounted these experiences to Bishop Mark Dyer at lunch one day at Virginia Theological Seminary not long after one of my visits home. Instead of a gentle word of encouragement, he challenged me brusquely, "She is still your mother, and she has much to teach you." I don't remember too much more about our conversation, but his stinging words began to penetrate my heart.

There was a definite change on my next visit home. I discovered that my mother's sense of humor that sparkled with mischievousness had shifted but still remained. We laughed over silly antics until my sides ached, and I remembered how she used laughter long ago to counter my adolescent angst. That night when she stood in silence at my door, I folded the covers back and motioned her into my bed. She lay down, took my hand, sighed, and then fell into a deep sleep. And yes, she still had much to teach me, if I would slow down, listen, and learn.—*Dorothy*

✳ ✳ ✳

Most of us are unprepared intellectually, emotionally, and spiritually for a diagnosis of Alzheimer's or a related disease in someone we love, much less in ourselves. Even as we watch the progression of dementia, we rationalize what we are seeing and how we respond. During this time, when we are overwhelmed with decisions that must be made, health issues to be confronted, and financial realities to be navigated, it is easy to lose sight of the person we are so focused on. At some point they also lose sight of us.

✳ ✳ ✳

My father, who had given me strength and wisdom all of my life, assumed I was his wife. His memories of my mother, who had been his wife for over fifty years, seemed to have faded away.

When we talk about our dad, my brother often calls him Norval, dad's given name. Naming him fleshes out his personality for us and ties the person we took care of at the end of his life to the man we knew as children and adults. My brother stopped seeing the "Norval" in our dad during the last months of his life. Like most caregivers, we didn't have much guidance for this new role into which we had been thrust. We hadn't read theology about the self or encountered the writing of people like Christine Bryden, a spokesperson for people like her who have dementia.

My brother recently told me that one of his biggest regrets was his inability to connect with Norval when he was with him toward the end of his life. "I think," said my brother, "as I look back at the last months of his life and all that he had to cope with, that Norval was simply doing the best he could." With all the confusion, uncertainty, and changes, Norval put on the best front possible.

Not long before he was moved to the memory unit, dad would look out the window of his high-rise retirement community and see a familiar Ford Mercury—the same type of car he had driven for years. Several times he gathered up his room key and wallet and headed outside. If the car door was locked, he tried in vain to get in. If it was unlocked, he would get in and just sit. The resident who owned the car was understandably upset by this intrusion.

The memory of dad's "break-ins" still makes us smile. But my brother and I realize now that Norval was still able to assert himself not only in commandeering this car, but also in the way he brought his own sense of order to a life that seemed so disordered. His sense of his "self" didn't diminish, although we were too muddled to see it ourselves.

Finding my dad's "self" often seemed beyond me as a weary caregiver. Between his confused mind and the cloudiness of my own clarity from increasing worry, the words of wisdom he was still capable of forming fell on deaf ears. Humor from car break-ins and his ability to laugh at himself were the antidotes that cleared the clouds for both of us.—*Dorothy*

✳ ✳ ✳

Holding Onto the Self

In chapter 1, we note that researchers have never identified one distinct part of the brain as a person's "self." It is not possible, therefore, for dementia to claim that self—or for any of us to lose that self despite the questions and uncertainty that arise from the reality of living with dementia. When Christine Bryden, a dementia advocate from Australia, speaks at conferences around the world about dealing with her own dementia, people attending her academic presentations, especially medical professionals, scoff at the idea that she has dementia. Bryden said in a presentation, "I seek to change these outsider views, which speak for me and about me, rather than letting me express verbally or non-verbally my continuing sense of self."[3]

We have been conditioned, maybe by the speed at which Alzheimer's disease affects the brain, to look for significant memory loss and an inability of people with dementia to function "normally." To overcome her own memory limitations, Bryden uses scripts and memory aids when she speaks about the scientific and theological implications of her dementia. Her message is complex, her language reflects complicated theories, and her delivery is flawless. And yet, during a session she attended at the conference, she slipped out for a moment, got completely lost, and returned forty-five minutes later with the help of strangers.

✳ ✳ ✳

Almost everyone who has met Christine Bryden, heard her lecture, or had a conversation with her is amazed by her candor and ability to look beyond her limitations. She was told she had dementia over twenty years ago and has the brain scans to prove it. Although the scans provide irrefutable evidence of her brain's diminished capacity, doctors and colleagues remain skeptical. Some "experts" who dismiss that diagnosis as false are unable to hear her words from their limited perspectives.

She has been a spokesperson for people with dementia since she got that diagnosis. During this time she met, fell in love with, and married her husband, Paul. She also recently completed the final requirements for a doctorate. Christine is not the average person with dementia, but she does transcend the condition, which gives her the freedom to risk, with courage, new horizons.

I met her at the seventh International Conference on Ageing and Spirituality in 2017 in Chicago. She had traveled with her husband from her home in Australia, and was still fighting jet lag when I had my first brief exchange with her. She warns new acquaintances that she will have no memory of their names or their conversations.

One of her passions is her love for her husband, which is mirrored in his love for her. Another of those passions is her understanding of her "self." She realizes that she has related to the world differently since her diagnosis, "but my subjective sense of self remains." She added, "I am far more than a deteriorating self in an increasingly empty shell of a body, with disappearing neurons and neuronal pathways."[4]

Her words brought to mind other words I've heard people say about those with dementia: "It's so sad to see someone stripped of her humanity." "There simply is no there, there." "He doesn't know if I visit or not." "All that is left is an empty shell."

Christine's life shows how shallow and untrue those observations are. Through her eyes, we see more clearly the power of self when we encounter someone with dementia. The resiliency we find generally in older people who do not have dementia is also apparent in those who do. There is a tender beauty and grace in the way those with dementia maintain the dignity of their "selves" that we fail to see when we make dismissive judgments about them.—*Dorothy*

✳ ✳ ✳

We need to listen to what we say about people with dementia. Our words will probably have no real impact on them, but when they bounce back at us, they stoke our fears and misconceptions. Caregivers, family, and friends of a person with dementia often report that their loved one seems to disappear with the progression of the disease. Our discussion of theology in chapters 3 and 4 argues that the factors that make us human go beyond rationality. Despite the Western, intellectual influence that molds our thoughts and opinions, rationality has its limits and does not define our "selves," or us, or our identity as beloved children of God.

Theologian David Keck calls Alzheimer's the "theological" disease because it affects memory, language, and the ability to plan the future, which many people believe make us human.[5] He believes that Alzheimer's erodes the essence of the self and decreases the personhood of those who have it. "The loss of memory entails a loss of self," writes Keck, "and we can no longer be secure in our notions of 'self-fulfillment.' Indeed, our entire sense of personhood and human purpose is challenged because we are dealing with the apparent disintegration of a human being."[6]

This unfortunate view may account for people not believing that their visit matters to the person with dementia: "She's not the same person" or "They won't remember that I was here anyway." It may account for why sometimes there is shame attached to the illnesses that cause dementia, and why even naming the diseases can sometimes be viewed as taboo. Theologian John Swinton argues that if we are our memories—if our sense of self is determined by what we can remember about the world and ourselves, then Keck is correct: losing memory eventually means losing self. However, writes Swinton, "human beings are much more than bundles of memories. The key in Keck's statement lies in the word *apparent*. There is a world of difference between an *apparent* dissolution of a human being and the *actual* dissolution of that person."[7] If we take the time to listen to people, writes Swinton, what we saw as *apparent* becomes more complex, opaque, and surprising.

> Devastating as dementia undoubtedly is, the human beings experiencing it do not dissolve. They are certainly changed, and there is much suffering and cause for lament. *But these people remain rightly held within the memories of God.* It is our ideas about what humanness, the nature of the self, and self-fulfillment mean that will have to be dissolved and re-created.[8]

Swinton believes that knowing *about* God may not be as important as *knowing* God, and "that knowing God involves much more than memory, intellect, and cognition."[9]

Notes

1. Sally Quinn, *Finding Magic* (New York: HarperOne, 2017).
2. Sally Quinn, "He was behaving differently. He had lost something. I was the only one who noticed," *Washington Post*, September 6, 2017, C-1.
3. Christine Bryden, "A Continuing Sense of Self within the Lived Experience of Dementia," presentation at the seventh International Conference on Ageing and Spirituality, June 4–7, 2017, Chicago, Illinois, accessed June 16, 2017, https://www.7thinternationalconference.org/copy-of-plenary-speakers.
4. Ibid.
5. David Keck, *Forgetting Whose We Are* (Nashville: Abingdon Press, 1996), 15.
6. Ibid.
7. John Swinton, *Dementia: Living in the Memories of God* (Grand Rapids, MI: William B. Eerdmans Publishing Company, 2012), 14.
8. Ibid., 15.
9. Ibid.

Introduction

And now that I am old and gray-headed, O God, do not forsake me,
Till I make known your strength to this generation
And your power to all who are to come . . .
You have showed me great troubles and adversities,
But you will restore my life
And bring me up again from the deep places of the earth. —Psalm 71[1]

God's promise is full of redemption of all things, and dementia is no exception. How can dementia that is so frightening and debilitating also be redeeming? As daughters of parents with dementia, our journey from despair to a place of hope has been long and often winding. We began it years ago when our parents entered a world of confusion, isolation, and loss brought on by Alzheimer's disease. As caregivers, our experiences ricocheted from despair to joy as we became bystanders in their new worlds. We discovered the redemptive power of God's grace and love over and over when we bumped into walls only to turn and find new paths. Often it was a parent who, despite a fog of confusion, showed us the way.

We discovered that learning about scientific breakthroughs in brain research gave us a deeper understanding of the changes we saw in our parents. We found that the words of theologians brought us insight and comfort through their messages of human dignity, redemption, and God's extraordinary love. Our faith deepened as our spiritual journeys went in new directions, challenging us to look for God's abundance even in the midst of loss and despair.

Not every visit with our parents was filled with insight. Like anyone else, they could be testy, cranky, demanding, tearful, stubborn, or resistant. The need to be in control of one's life does not just go away because a person has dementia. Watching logic disappear along with memories is never easy. When we were patient and listened well, there were redeeming moments that lifted us above our anger, fear, and frustration. Observations from our parents that plumbed the depth of their wisdom and experience surfaced when we least expected them.

Perhaps it is hindsight, but we have concluded that there is little doubt that new viewpoints on Alzheimer's and related dementias are needed to deal with these illnesses in more productive ways. With the numbers of people who live with dementia growing and no cure at present, it is important that we find the best ways to treat, support, and care for those who are suffering and those who support them. On a deeper level, we need to put the phenomenon of dementia into perspective. We need to look beyond the losses, interruptions, grief, and inconveniences of neurodegenerative diseases to discover God in our lives and our human resilience that surpasses our loss.

✳ ✳ ✳

When my mother's Alzheimer's disease had progressed to a point where she was unable to put sentences together, she said, seemingly out of the blue, "I'm still the same." It was clearly a monumental effort to articulate the sentence, so I paid deep attention. She was letting me know that she felt the same inside. I realized that we were experiencing not a loss of her "self," but rather something that was at least in part a communication issue. Because of this spiritual gift from my mother, I changed the way I looked at her illness and learned to patiently wait to see more. I saw spiritual aspects of my mother that were so profound that they greatly changed me. She could, at times, be very complex and lucid, despite her general reduced level of cognition. As a scientist, I wanted answers to questions that science could not yet address. As a student of theology, I was also searching for what the Church says about human dignity in the face of suffering and illness.—*Janice*

✳ ✳ ✳

Some of the problems we face with dementia-related illnesses can be seen in the following two stories:

＊ ＊ ＊

A chaplain at a large continuum of care community recently reported meeting a local parish clergyperson in the elevator of the facility. Making small talk, the chaplain asked him who he had come to visit and how the visits went. "Well, I have three members here," the pastor replied, "but two are out of it so I just said hello and left my card." Undoubtedly, this pastor will dutifully report to his church council that he made three pastoral calls.[2]

A hospital doctor is standing at the bedside of an elderly woman who has severe Alzheimer's. Her adult children are also present. He is talking about hospice care with the children. "What are you keeping her alive for?" he asks them, as if she were not awake or not in the room. Then he moves closely toward her face and shouts (she is not hard of hearing), "What do you do for fun, Jane?" She cannot answer, but grimaces.

＊ ＊ ＊

The first story shows there is a basic unease with visiting people with dementia—even for clergy—that is not unlike that experienced visiting those with other mental or physical disabilities. This is why it is important to have a basic scientific understanding of illnesses with symptoms of dementia. This background removes prejudices that the person is malingering or is at fault in some way. No one knows what causes Alzheimer's disease or the related dementias. Scientific knowledge decreases the stigma of these diseases by helping us to see that it is a disease of the brain—nothing more and nothing less. Those who have diseases of some other organ, such as the heart or kidney, are not stigmatized, so why do we single out diseases of the brain? Scientific knowledge can be used to devise ways to increase communications with a person with dementia, such as knowing how the senses serve communication. For example, brain science is beginning to explain why music often reaches people with advanced dementia.

The second story shows that prejudice—even those of medical personnel—can severely harm people with dementia and their families. Bioethicist Stephen Post suggests that the stigma concerning dementia results from our society's overvaluation of rationality.[3] Whether it is due to their physical or mental limitations, a person with dementia is marginalized, and often their caregivers are pushed aside as well. The lack of respect for the "self" of the vulnerable patient is countered by arguments of many modern theologians and ethicists. A basic theological grounding and understanding of the illnesses lead to a treatment of people that maintains their full worth and wholeness. The person still holds a role in the context of his or her family and community. Others may hold important parts of their memory for them, but the person herself is entitled to exist and to be treated fully as a person until the end of her life.

Why This Book

There are 47 million people in the world who have Alzheimer's disease and related dementias, with nearly 10 million new cases each year.[4] Without a cure, this number is expected to grow to 132 million by 2050. In the U.S., currently 70 percent are living at home and most have mild to moderate dementia. You probably see them every day and don't realize it. To a certain extent they can function at home and in society with the help of family and other care partners.

The growing challenge of caring for this large number puts great strain on society's medical and financial resources as well as on caregivers' time and livelihood. Medical and care costs worldwide were estimated in 2015 at $818 billion, which is 1.1 percent of the global gross domestic product, a large fraction for a single issue. According to the World Health Organization (WHO), the 2030 cost projection of two trillion dollars threatens economic development globally and could overwhelm health and social services. In its May 2017 report, "Global action plan on the public health response to dementia 2017–2025," WHO urges national and international partners to work to increase awareness of dementia, establish dementia-friendly initiatives, accelerate research and innovation, and increase support for caregivers.

Redeeming Dementia aims to provide a deeper vocabulary about dementia to raise awareness and insight among the faithful and enable them to better cope and advocate for themselves, loved ones, parishioners, or other people who suffer from dementia. We will provide ways to embrace those living with dementia as well as their families and to help alleviate stigma. And we will challenge readers to find new ways of knowing God by embracing the "self" of all people, especially those who have dementia.

How to Read This Book

Organized first around the three themes of science, theology, and spirituality, the book then ends by focusing on how congregations can respond to people with dementia in their midst. The major parts of the book can be read in any order. Throughout the text we share personal stories from others as well as ourselves. Each chapter concludes with reflection questions as a way to emphasize what is important and perhaps controversial, and to give you a chance to reflect on your own stories and to take them further, either in a group or individually.

Chapter 1 begins by discussing the physical aspects of the healthy brain. It appears to be a coincidence that dementia-causing illnesses are spiking at a time when brain science is undergoing an exciting revolution. There is a new appreciation of the complexity of the human brain and its role in our evolution as a species. It is far more complicated than we realized. One human brain contains 100,000 miles of fiber, long enough to go around the earth four times. The potential capacity of the human brain has been estimated to equal the power of the entire Internet. New instrumentation and data-based approaches, as well as ideas about computation and consciousness, are producing some of the most rapid changes seen in any scientific field of our day.

The body is important in the Christian story and in the arguments here. Concepts such as the "self," "consciousness," and "spirituality" that were previously conjectures by philosophers and theologians are now aspects that researchers are beginning to measure. Important recent discoveries about memory, the senses, sleep, and aging add to the evolving picture of the healthy brain. At the same time, with all the advances in imaging, there is no one area in the brain identified as the "self" or "spirituality."

The media often write about breakthroughs in brain research and dementia. The terminology in this first chapter will help you to read and digest those reports with more clarity. Perhaps more importantly, we believe a scientific understanding of the brain gives us hope, not only for a potential cure, but also for the awesome capacity of this extraordinary human organ.

Chapter 2 explains the latest scientific understanding of dementia as a symptom of various diseases that cause degeneration of brain cells and, therefore, interrupt connections in the brain that form the basis of central tasks such as memory, learning, and executive functions. The stages of Alzheimer's disease are described, with an emphasis on what *remains* at each stage. Even in advanced Alzheimer's, much of the brain is still working. Billions of pieces of information per second about vision, hearing, smells, touch, taste, and more are still being transmitted, perhaps not as well as before but usually still working. We do not know what the person is experiencing, and we should not presume. Again, there is no evidence that the diseases causing dementia destroy the "self" or "spirituality."

In chapter 3, we turn to theology about the human person to lay the groundwork for our response to dementia. Historically, the concept of rationality was central in explaining how humans differ from other higher animals. But this single criterion is problematic when it comes to people with dementia. When a person develops dementia, are they less of a person? Do they lose their connection to God? By citing contemporary theologians who are broadening concepts about what makes us human, we strongly answer "no" to these questions. David Kelsey believes human beings are who they are because of the way God relates to them. The basis for the value and relationship of the human being lies in God—that is, outside the human being themselves. Since this is mostly about divine characteristics, the relationship and therefore personhood are not affected by dementia or any human illness.

Chapter 4 applies several concepts of Kelsey's theology of the human person to the case of dementia. We are the glory of God—even if mute or paralyzed or lacking rationality. The most fundamental thing about us, Kelsey says, is our basic personal identity as grounded in God, not our everyday identity or health status. This chapter also cites other theologians writing on disability and dementia.

Chapter 5 focuses on aging in general, recognizing that most people with dementia are also facing the changes and losses of old age. The spiritual life is not disconnected from the changes that aging brings to bodies, including health and emotional stability. Depression and substance abuse are a reality for many older people coping with physical changes, financial challenges, and difficult decisions that have no easy answers. Gerontologist Elaine Brody wrote when she was eighty-six that she was ready for old age intellectually but not emotionally. "Common experiences of old age, such as illness and losses, were unexpected, even though expectable."[5] At the same time, recent studies that measure happiness show that well-being increases with age, with older people outscoring younger people by a sizable margin.[6] Time is actually on their side as professional and personal demands lessen, giving them space to bring *being* rather than constant *doing* back into their consciousness. Supported by family and a community of faith, many older people embrace a new rhythm in their lives that leads to satisfaction and even joy.

Chapter 6 begins our discussion of what congregations can do to meet the challenges of dementia. Because the onset of dementia is often slow and difficult to detect, family and caregivers may be reluctant to share the information with others. Even though help may be desperately needed, many won't ask for it—even those who are long-term members of a congregation. Ironically, a faith community can ease the transitions we all face in life. Donald F. Clingan, who was instrumental in bringing the heritage of religion and spirituality into the field of gerontology, wrote, "Spiritual resiliency is nurtured in community. It is the experience of being knocked down and stunned by events and finding a hand of comfort, support, and encouragement that assists us in once again rising. It is the experience of faith, hope, and love shared through our various connections in life that nurtures our inner renewal."[7] Helping congregations understand dementia and giving them tools for communications and hospitality can lead to the full participation of those with dementia and their caregivers in community life. People with dementia keep reminding us that we need to be creating solutions *with* them rather than *for* them. They have much to teach us if we will only listen and pay attention.

How can congregations and other spiritual groups serve those with dementia? One of the challenges is that people with dementia and those who care for them tend to be isolated. Often due to misunderstandings about dementia and lack of knowledge about how to interact, friends and extended family pull back, creating a real deficit in the person's life. This has a negative effect in two aspects decreasing the person's well-being through grief about the losses of family and friends, and increasing fear on the part of the distancing friends. This fear can give rise to a stigmatizing attitude toward dementia.

Chapter 7 offers a variety of ways that congregations can get involved to serve those with dementia and their families. Following the Dementia-Friendly Church movement in England, congregations can hold special worship services, which can nurture the spiritual growth of people with dementia, as well as caregivers. They can also start a Memory Café, an informal get-together of those with dementia and their families that provides a relaxing respite from what might be an isolated care situation at home or more clinical environments. Memory cafés have been reported to reduce feelings of loneliness and increase quality of life.

Congregations and spiritual groups can provide people with dementia the opportunity to share their talents through service as appropriate, including participating in liturgy for as long as possible, accompanied by another person if needed. Providing a respite partner during services allows the caregiver to focus on worship, and also creates a meaningful ministry for volunteers. Individuals and congregations can also join with other efforts, such as the Stephen Ministry and Community of Hope International, as well as efforts by professional societies, medical staff, care facilities, hospitals, and governmental agencies, including the Dementia Friendly America movement. Finally, advocacy on behalf of those living with dementia and their caregivers is another possible role for congregations.

Our hope for this book is that reflecting on the scientific, theological, and spiritual aspects of dementia will lead to helpful insights that will eventually shift some of the focus about these illnesses from devastation, dehumanization, and loss to an embrace of the selfhood, coping, and spiritual gifts that come from any challenge before us. In the long run, we hope for better inclusion and care for people with dementia and their families and friends in our society, especially the empowerment of congregations to continue ministry through the end of life.

Notes

1. The Book of Common Prayer (New York: The Church Hymnal Corporation, 1979), 684.
2. Susan H. McFadden, Mandy Ingram, and Carla Baldauf, "Actions, Feelings, and Values: Foundations of Meaning and Personhood in Dementia," *Journal of Religious Gerontology* 11 (2001): 3-4, 67-86.

3. Stephen G. Post, *The Moral Challenge of Alzheimer's Disease* (Baltimore: The Johns Hopkins University Press, 1995), 3.
4. World Health Organization, accessed January 10, 2018, http://www.who.int /mediacentre/factsheets/fs362/en/.
5. Elaine M. Brody, "On Being Very, Very Old: An Insider's Perspective," *The Gerontologist* 50, no. 1 (February 2010): 2-10, doi.org/10.1093/geront/gnp143.
6. *State of American Well-Being: State Well-Being Rankings for Older Americans.* Gallup-Healthway Well-Being Index, 2015, accessed December 27, 2017, http://www.well-beingindex.com/hubfs/Well-Being_Index/2014_Data /Gallup-Healthways_State_of_American_Well-Being_Older_Americans _Rankings.pdf?t=1508795566327.
7. Donald Clingan, "Foreword," in James A. Thorson, ed., *Perspectives on Spiritual Well-Being and Aging* (Springfield, IL: Charles C. Thomas Publisher LTD., 2000), xiii.

CHAPTER 1

The Healthy Brain

The body is very important in our story. Christians believe in the Incarnation, that the second person of the Trinity assumed human form in the person of Jesus Christ. We are embodied, too. This chapter begins our discussion about the physical body, and in particular, the healthy brain.

Brain and Mind

Many today believe that it is the human brain that makes us different from other forms of life. It is immense and more complex in comparison to that of other species, giving rise to an unprecedented human consciousness with abilities such as self-awareness, intelligence, language, self-control, extensive planning, emotion, the ability to cooperate, and other attributes observed only to a lesser degree, if at all, in the species closest to us. Rather than believing in the traditional concept of the soul, some theologians believe that it is consciousness,[1] or the "information pattern,"[2] that survives after death. (See chapter 3 for more information on this topic.)

Those holding to the scientific-secular model for what makes us human would say that it was the surging size of the brain about two hundred thousand years ago that marked the transition from human ancestors to human beings that were largely like us.³ Because the brain is affected by dementia, those characteristics that some believe make us human can also be affected. This is why theologian David Keck referred to Alzheimer's disease as the "theological disease," because it calls into question beliefs about what makes us human.⁴

Another layer of the theological and scientific discussion is about the subtle differences between brain and mind. For the purposes of our discussion, *brain* is the physical organ made of brain cells (neurons), fed by circulating fluids and chemicals, full of energy, which as a system generates electrochemical signals. The brain is an object you could hold in your hand. The *mind* includes intangibles such as thoughts, processing, perceptions, emotions, spirituality, and even relationships. The mind is like the software, yielding laws and theories, yes, but also changing in time and difficult to categorize.

Jeannette Norden articulates the common belief among neuroscientists that "the brain is the biological substrate [substance] of the mind."⁵ To complicate matters, it has been discovered that the human heart has forty thousand neurons, and the gut has a billion neurons,⁶ so even the physical organ "brain" may not be as contained (just in our heads) as we once thought.

Basics about the Brain and Neurons

The 3-pound human brain is much more complex than previously thought. It consists of 100 billion neurons—brain cells—packed together in a consistency like that of firm tofu. The human brain uses a very large amount (20 percent) of your body's energy when you are at rest. The brain has two hemispheres and all but one of the substructures are paired left and right. The figure on the next page shows a slice through the brain from the forehead to the back of the head, revealing one hemisphere.

There are three major parts of the brain. The brain stem includes the spinal cord, cerebellum (which controls balance and rote motions), and medulla oblongata (which controls heart rate, blood pressure, and breathing, among other activities). It is called the stem because it connects to the rest of our body, as if the brain were the fruit. The brain stem is evolutionarily the oldest part that we share in common with animals. In addition to the functions already named, it is also responsible for digestion, reflexes, sleeping, and arousal. It is the first to develop in a fetus, and the last to be affected by Alzheimer's.

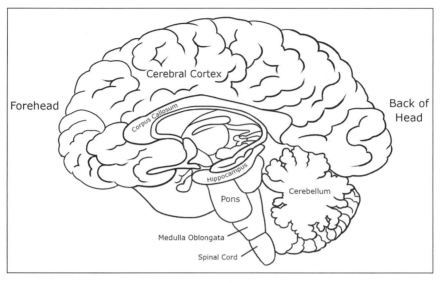

Diagram of slice through the brain from forehead (left) to back of head (right) revealing one hemisphere.

The second part, the midbrain, is the emotional brain, regulating sex hormones, sleep cycle, hunger, emotions, and addictions. The midbrain also contains the pleasure center that makes us feel good, and the amygdala, which is responsible for the fight-or-flight impulse, anger, and fear. The hippocampus—the name in Greek means "seahorse" because it was imagined to resemble such an animal—is thought to consolidate short-term memory into long-term memory and enable spatial memory. The hippocampus is the first place that is affected by Alzheimer's, which is why the first symptoms of this disease are usually loss of short-term memory, difficulty forming new memories, and disorientation in space.

The third part of the brain is the wrinkly, folded exterior, the cerebral cortex (or cerebrum), which is the thinking brain. It is evolutionarily the newest part, and in humans its size is massive compared to in other animals. Whereas a mouse brain is 40 percent cerebral cortex, a human brain is 80 percent.[7] Here is the seat of our thoughts, reasoning, language, planning, and imagination. Parts of the cerebral cortex also process our senses, temperature, movement, reading, music, and mathematics. It is affected in the middle and late stages of dementia.

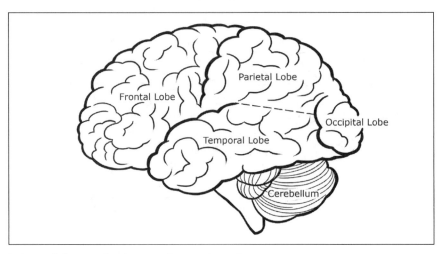

Lobes of the cerebral cortex (or cerebrum).

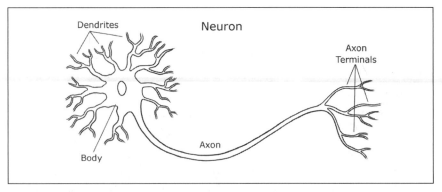

Diagram of a brain cell (neuron), usually microscopic in size (the size of the cross section of a human hair).

The cerebral cortex is divided into four lobes. The frontal lobe is responsible for executive functions such as concentration, planning, and problem-solving. The parietal lobe is associated with understanding speech and using words. The temporal lobe interprets sensory stimuli and contains memory of visual and auditory patterns. The occipital lobe interprets visual information and recognizes visual images.

Of the 100 billion neurons making up the brain, there are thousands of different kinds: multipolar, unipolar, bipolar, pyramidal, and so on. Most have a microscopic cell body, a long projection (or fiber) called the axon, and dendritic terminals, like tree branches, that connect with nearby neurons. Axons are usually microscopic but can be as long as several feet, reaching down the spinal cord to activate muscles, for example.

The cell bodies gather to form substructures, called gray matter because of their gray coloring. The axons join to form adjoining layers called white matter, so named because the axons are coated with a waxy protective substance called myelin, which appears white. There are an astounding 100,000 miles of axonal fibers in one human brain, enough to circle the Earth four times.[8]

A method called diffusion spectrum imaging, invented only in the past few years, produced the image shown in the figure below, which reveals a grid-like order of the fibers that astounded even most neuroscientists. Most expected a more tangled anatomy.

In addition to neurons, the brain also has as many *glial cells* that provide support for neurons, such as cleaning their environments. We will see later

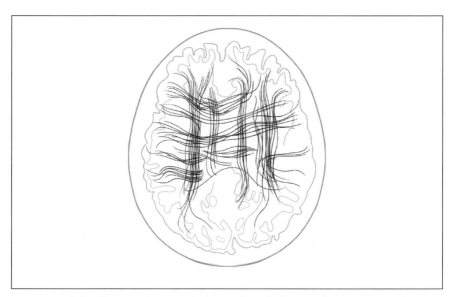

Drawing of the fiber pathways of a living female human brain, mapped noninvasively with diffusion spectrum imaging. The image shows a view from above (front of the brain is at the top of the picture). The fibers of white matter (axons of brain cells) are arranged in major grid-like pathways.[9]

on how this is an important process during sleep and is possibly a point of deficiency in illnesses causing dementia.

The Brain as an Electrochemical System

Feelings, thoughts, sensations, and muscle actions all are thought to result from particular neural pathways involving neurons and chemical changes. Neurons communicate by sending electrical pulses that travel down their axons. The rate of the pulses—faster or slower—and the intensity of the pulses—strong or weak—contain the information the brain is trying to transfer. The pulses stimulate the release of chemicals (neurotransmitters), which travel a short distance from one cell to the next across *synapses*, passing the signal and wiring the two cells together. It's been said that "neurons that fire together, wire together."[10] This concept of networking among cells is thought to be important in memory as well as in many other brain processes.

The neurotransmitters released at the synapses have various effects. Some, for example, are excitatory—triggering wakefulness, attentiveness, anger,

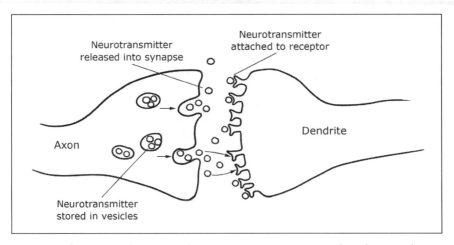

Diagram of a neuronal synapse showing neurotransmitters (dots) leaving the end of the neuron on the left as the result of an electrical pulse that came down the axon, and becoming attached to receptors on the dendrite of the neuron on the right, creating the pulses in that neuron to pass on the information.

aggression, etc.—while others are inhibitory—calming anxiety, inducing sleep, etc.

With electrical signals traveling all of the possible synapses in the many neurons and the many chemicals involved, the agility of the brain is enormous. The brain has potentially forty quadrillion synaptic connections, making one human brain potentially more powerful than the entire Internet (that is, a storage potential of one petabyte.)[11]

Neurotransmitter receptors are not just restricted to the brain, but rather are found throughout the body. Neuropsycho-immunologists Candace Pert and Michael Ruff termed this "a network of communication between brain and body"[12] or, colloquially, "liquid brain." This fact, together with the knowledge that the heart and gut have neurons of their own, shows that the information system in our body extends beyond the boundaries of what we traditionally call the brain.

Neurotransmitter	Functions
Acetylcholine	excites cells activates muscles wakefulness
Glutamate	helps learning assists memory
GABA	slows down and regulates anxiety
Endorphins	reduce pain increase pleasure
Dopamine	provides motivation gives pleasure
Epinephrine (adrenaline)	maintains alertness energizes
Serotonin	regulates body temperature, memory, emotion, sleep, appetite, and mood
Oxytocin (found during labor and in breast milk)	elicits "motherly" love elicits romantic love increases trust

A few of the major types of neurotransmitters in the brain and their functions.

The interaction of the mind and body has been a philosophical quandary at least since Ancient Greece. Pert's contemporary neuroscientific description of "liquid brain" recalls Gregory of Nyssa's description in 300 CE: "the mind approaching our nature in some inexplicable and incomprehensible way, and coming into contact with it, is to be regarded as both in it and around it, neither implanted in it nor enfolded with it, but in a way which we cannot speak or think."[13]

It is natural that some of the first therapies for dementia focus on the brain chemicals that can affect brain activity. One common Alzheimer's medication, Aricept (donepezil), increases acetylcholine in the brain to increase activity. Namenda (memantine) is thought to block excess glutamate that can kill neurons.

Long ago we were taught in school that once the brain reaches maturity, it no longer makes new neurons, but in 1998 Peter Eriksson showed this is wrong: the brain does make new neurons in some areas.[14] A chemical named brain-derived neurotrophic factor (BDNF) causes brain cells to grow. How do we increase BDNF? Arthur Kramer and Kirk Erickson demonstrated in 2011 that physical exercise increases the size of the hippocampus and improves memory.[15]

Other studies also indicate the brain can be altered even into adulthood in a process termed neuroplasticity. This includes forming new substructures on the neurons (e.g., spines), new connections between neurons (synapses), and new receptors on neuron surfaces. For example, researchers believe that the brain can remap and rewire in response to injury and training. Yet the assignment of brain regions to functions is thought to be fairly stable. Rodrigo Quian Quiroga found that one particular neuron fired when a patient was shown different photographs of television actress Jennifer Aniston, but not for photographs of others. Quiroga suggests that it is the abstract identity that is stored and that there may be an "invariant, sparse and explicit code."[16] He suggests the situation is likely more complicated than a one-to-one correspondence between a face and a neuron, but the result indicates certain stability between function and structure. It is still the early days of research in understanding structure, function, and memory in the brain.

The Senses

The five senses of vision, hearing, smell, taste, and touch increase the richness of our interaction with the world. Each is an immeasurable gift not only helping our survival but also yielding sensual pleasures like the appreciation of beauty. As inputs to the brain, the senses are vital for communication. To communicate most effectively with a person with dementia, it is helpful to understand what is happening with each of the senses, as they might be altered with the illness.

Touch is the first sense in a newborn, and often the last to be lost to dementia. Our bodies are covered with a network of six to ten million sensors; more than half of those sensors are located on our hands, feet, and faces. Where possible and with permission, touch is an important, pastoral way to communicate. A light touch on the shoulder or holding hands can be very effective. If a person is lying down, touching the feet can also be effective. Passive touch, like the sun or breeze on bodies and faces, is also a pleasure that is not to be underestimated.

With the sense of smell, the signal pathway is a direct line to the brain, separated by just two or three synapses to the hippocampus. This is why smells can be quickly and strongly associated with memories and emotions. We can harness the power of smell in liturgies through the use of incense, for example, or use specific smells through aromatherapy to benefit particular symptoms. A 2002 study showed that the scent of lemon balm significantly decreased agitation in people with severe dementia.[17] In some cases, however, dementia sufferers may experience a loss of smell.[18]

Through the sense of vision, retinal cells transmit one billion pieces of information to the brain every second. The brain then has to sort through this astounding amount of information to decide what to pay attention to. People tend to pay more attention to *changes* in their visual field. Because people with Alzheimer's often lose peripheral vision, it is important to approach a person from the front rather than the side. Getting eye contact before speaking is also important. People with Alzheimer's may lose contrast between colors and cannot see blue and purple tones. Using red, orange, and yellow will enhance contrast for clearer vision.

The ear has the fewest sensory cells of any sensory organ, only about 3,500. People with dementia may have hearing loss, similarly to any person who is aging. If a person's response is lagging, however, it may not be a hearing issue, but rather a longer processing time. Shouting at people with dementia won't shorten that processing time. Professionals suggest that directions or questions be as short and simple as possible, followed by thirty seconds of waiting. By waiting, an answer may come.

Memory and Forgetting

Memory is everywhere. We are often asked, "Do you remember this?" When we are with family or old friends, we hear ourselves say, "Remember when . . . ?" Even in church we are told, "Do this in remembrance of me."

Memory is required for our identities, learning, relationships, and decision-making. Photographs and souvenirs memorialize holidays, vacations, and special celebrations. National observances and monuments help us remember critical events in our history. Forgetfulness is also everywhere. In our busy lives, we cling to calendars to boost our memories. We want to remember the intense feelings from joyous moments of our lives—falling in love, recovering from a serious illness, the birth of a child. We tend to think deeply about memory only when it lapses and serious problems start to infringe on our everyday lives. These lapses could be due to medication, stress, or illness, but we most fear an irreversible degenerative brain disease such as Alzheimer's disease.

While not completely understood, the resulting neural pathways consisting of hundreds of neurons may be the basis of long-term memory. When cells fire together, there is a chemical trace left behind called "long-term potentiation." The repetition of information during study, for example, strengthens these pathways, resulting in easier recall.

There is more than one kind of memory. Memory begins when our senses feed stimuli to our brains, many of which are ignored. When we pay attention, *sensory memory* is retained almost automatically, taking less than a second.[19] The information goes into *short-term memory*, which is like a temporary scratch pad. Short-term memory is a nerve impulse, not a well-worn track, and can hold about seven items for ten to fifteen seconds or sometimes up to one minute. The information can be quickly lost if more information comes in. The hippocampus (located in the figure on page 3) coordinates the conversion of short-term memory to long-term memory, functioning like a memory control center. For example, a childhood memory of a worship service might have sounds, smells, and emotions stored in their respective parts of the brain. The hippocampus ties these together from various parts of the brain (auditory, olfactory, emotional) to form a single episode.

Transfer to long-term memory occurs in a few seconds and is aided by repetition or by adding meaning or association. This is why recalling the name of someone new is easier if you repeat the name and associate it with another person you know.

Long-term memory is robust. In a healthy brain, the ability to recall may degrade, but memories remain intact. Long-term memory can be conscious (explicit), such as episodic memories of what you had for lunch or experiences such as your first kiss. These generally have associated feelings. Memories with a lot of emotion tend to last a long time. For example, many remember clearly what they were doing on September 11, 2001, but few remember what they were doing the day before that. We store our autobiography through long-term memory, orchestrated by the hippocampus.

Conscious memory also includes semantic memory, which is a collection of facts with no feelings or memories attached, such as the multiplication

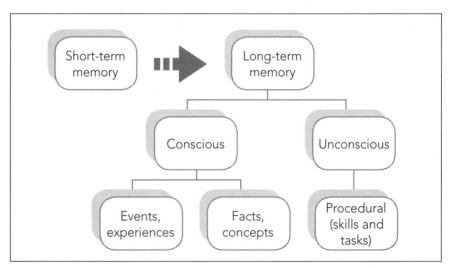

Types of memory

tables. Long-term memory can also be unconscious (implicit), including procedures, skills, and tasks such as riding a bike, tying a shoelace, reading a clockface, or playing the piano, requiring little thought to perform.

Different types of long-term memory are stored in different regions of the brain. Conscious long-term memory involves the hippocampus plus other areas throughout the brain. Procedural memories do not involve the hippocampus but rather are stored in motor control areas of the brain. Amee Baird and Séverine Samson found that a musician with Alzheimer's, for example, can still play the piano (using their unconscious procedural memory), but cannot recognize familiar melodies, which involves conscious memory.[20]

* * *

Mr. Polanski was a neighbor in my mother's memory care facility. His daughter and I first met while talking about Polish food, and then I learned that her father had played piano every Saturday night in a Polish club for over thirty years. A widower, Mr. Polanski had a cheerful disposition and a charming smile. He sometimes recognized his family, but due to Alzheimer's he required 24-7 care. The residents, who were mostly women, enjoyed his weekly piano performances, where for an hour he masterfully played and sang old songs with a joy that was felt by all.—*Janice*

* * *

What is forgetting? For short-term memory, it means that a nerve impulse has ceased being transmitted through a particular neural network. For long-term memory, it means that the synaptic connection among the neurons in a network becomes weakened. The structure that was modified decays because of a random event or because the cells that have the chemical information die through illness. Another possibility is that the hippocampus that recreates the episode from information in different parts of the brain is damaged. The memories may still be there, but not accessible.

Even the healthy brain prunes itself, getting rid of connections not often used, thus the phrase, "Use it or lose it." There is evidence that brain gym exercises (for example BrainHQ from Posit Science) help keep the mind active.

Sleep and Memory

The biological reasons for sleep and dreaming are not fully understood and are still being debated. From an evolutionary point of view, the loss of consciousness during sleep puts a person or animal at very high risk in terms of safety. Because humans need a significant amount of daily sleep, it must be extremely important. What does sleep have to do with memory?

There are two main theories about the purpose of sleep. During the phase of sleep known as rapid eye movement (REM), the hippocampus shows synchronized waves that some believe is memory consolidation.[21] The second, discovered only in the past few years, is about cleaning. Glial cells clean out all the molecular toxins and metabolites that build up from thinking and learning functions during the day.[22] These helper cells remove the excess proteins that are thought to be linked to Alzheimer's disease. Sleep is important for both memory consolidation and the removal of unwanted proteins. Dementia is associated with disturbed sleep, but we don't know if the lack of sleep contributes to the illness or if the illness disrupts sleep.

Sleep researchers recommend sleeping eight to nine hours daily. Naps should be ninety minutes in duration to complete an entire sleep cycle to maximize the cleaning function. If ninety minutes isn't possible, researchers recommend a twenty-minute nap as a good alternative for getting some rest.

The Long-Term Memory of Music

In the best and worst of times, music reaches our hearts in ways that other communication cannot. Alice Parker says, "Song is a right and a need."[23] Music obviously involves the auditory areas of the brain, but also taps into its emotional center. It boosts endorphins and other feel-good molecules that can lift spirits and even cause euphoria. The whole brain is involved when we listen to music. For nonmusicians, the right hemisphere is dominant for appreciation of melody and harmony and the left for rhythm and language. People who dance or play an instrument use even more of the brain, for example, the motor system that controls movements and coordination.

✳ ✳ ✳

I was fortunate to be able to observe a worship group led by a chaplain with six women with moderate to advanced dementia. When the a capella singing began, many of the women, though not fluid in conversation, could sing all the verses of familiar hymns, many more than I could. These verses were probably memorized when they were young. Especially popular among this group were "Amazing Grace," "Holy Holy Holy," "How Great Thou Art," "What a Friend We Have in Jesus," "Mine Eyes Have Seen the Glory," "Sweet Hour of Prayer," "Fairest Lord Jesus," and "Blessed Assurance."—*Janice*

* * *

There are several famous videos of people with advanced dementia who are uncommunicative but then become animated and talkative, reacting happily when hearing beloved music.[24, 25] These effects can last for hours or days and can stimulate memories. A 2015 study focused on how musical memory from people's youth can be preserved even in the case of advanced Alzheimer's. The researchers arranged for people in their late twenties to hear music from their youth while their brains were scanned. The scans revealed the primary area for long-term musical memory, superimposed on the brain sketch in Scan A on the next page.[26] This same area is surprisingly spared in the brains of those with Alzheimer's, as shown in Scan B.

A lesson for anyone visiting someone with Alzheimer's: play music from the person's youth, including hymns, Top Ten hits, oldies, and popular tunes.

The Self from a Neuroscientific Point of View

Despite all the neuroscientific research gains of the past decades, scientists have not identified a part of the brain that is the center of self or "soul." Modern neuroscience has shown progress in understanding both the anatomy and some of the function of the human brain. This has led to therapies for addiction, strokes, depression, trauma, seizures, tumors, dementia, and other major brain diseases. Yet even the most recent map of the brain[27] shows no one part that is associated with "self." A journal editor writes:

Most of us share a strong intuition that our own self is an irreducible whole, that there must be some place in our brains where our perceptions

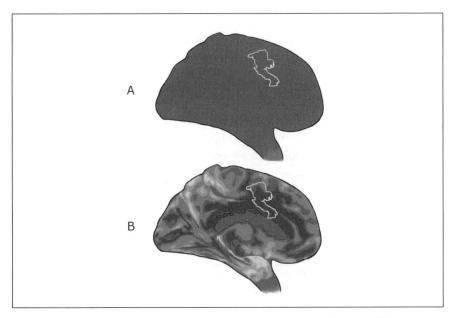

Drawing based on brain scans from a study on memory of music.[28] Scan A shows the area of the brain that correlates with long-term memory of music. Scan B shows Alzheimer's damage based on gray matter atrophy. The lighter areas represent more damage, and the darker areas less or no damage. It can be seen that the musical memory area corresponds to an area that has no to low Alzheimer's damage.

and thoughts all come together and where our future actions are decided. Yet this view is now known to be incorrect—different mental processes are mediated by different brain regions, and there is nothing to suggest the existence of any central controller.[29]

When you wake up in the morning, how do you know it's you? There are structures that are associated with parts of what we call "self."[30] The hippocampus handles experiences and stories and, therefore, our autobiography. In the midbrain, our amygdala and emotional system unconsciously act on our behavior and shape who we think we are. This includes our demeanor, emotional temperature, tendency to worry or get angry, and how we find pleasure. The cerebral cortex establishes who we think we are because it is the seat of thought and, in addition, our likes and dislikes.

Further subdivisions contribute to the "self" in specific ways. The prefrontal cortex originates our thoughts, plans, imagination, and ability to solve problems. The orbitofrontal cortex gives us goals, as well as a sense of morality and ethics, and is possibly the seat of conscience. The posterior parietal cortex is associated with distinguishing self from non-self; it is thought to establish the borders of the self. The temporal lobe allows us to recognize scenes and objects, and to process sounds and language. There are particular structures for recognizing faces.[31] Our talents—music, art, and sports, for example—which are in various parts of the brain, also constitute part of who we think we are. Because there is no one part of the brain that defines "self," there is no evidence that dementia can destroy our "self."

By studying brain-damaged subjects who experienced unconsciousness or coma, neuroscientists have identified some of the physical structures that correlate with consciousness. They ascertained that areas of the thalamus and cerebral cortex are associated with awareness, attention, and self-reference.[32] A "crown of thorns"–shaped cell that wraps continuously around the brain of a mouse was recently discovered. The authors propose that it is a tantalizing candidate for a linkage to consciousness because of its unusual circular shape and apparent connections to sensory inputs and outputs, but this is only a conjecture at this point.[33]

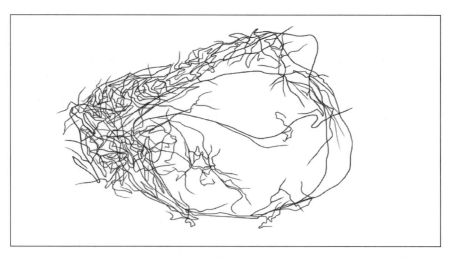

A giant neuron from a mouse's brain that is a continuous loop around the circumference of the brain. The authors named this the "Crown of Thorns Neuron."

Understanding why humans have subjective experiences is even more challenging. It is straightforward to understand how red light can be absorbed by the eye, resulting in a signal that travels to the brain and that the brain learns to call "red." What is not understood is why the person *experiences* the color red. This is an example of "qualia," the person's subjective experience associated with stimulation to the brain. Norden writes, "it is challenging to examine why consciousness appears to be 'something' that is happening to a 'me.' "[34]

Spirituality from a Neuroscientific Point of View

✳ ✳ ✳

At a time in the progression of her Alzheimer's when my mother was no longer articulating sentences, she once said (with perfect fluidity), "I know he knows me." I could only make sense of this if the "he" referred to God. Despite what we would characterize as her condition of chaotic confusion, to be so certain and lucid that God knew her was an astounding pronouncement. I was in awe at the quality of her aliveness and wondered what experience had moved mom to say this.—*Janice*

✳ ✳ ✳

Before it was possible to image the brain, researchers articulated two radically different hypotheses about spiritual experiences. The first is that no signal would show up in the brain because a spiritual experience occurs at the soul level, not the brain level. The second is that a specific module in the brain exists for spiritual experience that evolved for psychological evolutionary reasons. While it is early in this research, it appears that both hypotheses are incorrect.

Like the "self," spirituality is an experience that is not localized to one place but is found throughout the brain. Andrew Newberg and other neurotheologians have attempted to "measure" spirituality in the brain by searching for correlations between spiritual experiences and brain data. Whether they are observing monks meditating or nuns performing centering prayer during a brain scan, there is a consistent but distributed set of brain structures that change during these spiritual experiences. No one has identified a clear substructure that is the internal "cell phone" to God. Some areas of the brain that show an increase in activity ("light up") during spiritual experiences are associated with focus and emotion. But interestingly, significant *decreases* in activity are also noted. The observed decrease in activity in the posterior parietal cortex, which creates the boundary between self and others, could account for the feeling of unity with the world and/or God.[35] According to Newberg, sudden decreases in the frontal and parietal lobes are associated with "incredible shifts of perception and experiences of unity consciousness."[36] He proposes, "When the frontal lobe activity drops suddenly and significantly, logic and reason shut down, everyday consciousness is suspended, allowing other brain centers to experience the world in intuitive and creative ways."[37] One of the challenges of the research, practitioners report, is that spiritual experiences are not uniform and each type could result in a different brain signature. Further, the measurements are state of the art and sophisticated but still limited in capturing information; for example, it is not yet possible to map neurotransmitter patterns. While the scans capture some physical changes in the brain, it is by no means clear that this is all that is happening.

The idea that spiritual experiences are correlated with a decrease in brain activity, as if the brain in its resting state is throttling down something, is very interesting. Irene Cristofori studied Vietnam veterans who had bullet wounds in their brains and attempted to correlate their level of spirituality with the location of the wounds.[38] The idea is that the area of the brain that is wounded would "permanently" have less activity. The study is the first of its kind and is notable for having a large sample (116 persons with brain injury and 32 healthy controls). They measured spirituality using the M-scale standardized survey, which includes "the experience of profound unity with all that exists, a felt sense of sacredness, a sense of the experience of truth and reality at a fundamental level, deeply felt positive mood, transcendence of time and space, and difficulty explaining the experience in words."[39] Of those veterans routinely having the most spiritual experiences (highest M-scale scores), it is astounding that the brain damage was in similar areas, located in the front of the brain (just behind the forehead) in the dorsolateral prefrontal cortex (dlPFC), as shown in the following figure.[40]

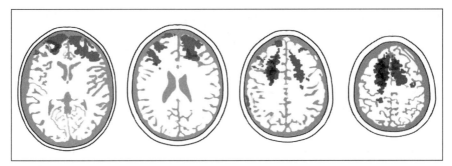

The cross-sectional scans of the entire brain are shown averaged for fourteen patients with the highest M scores. The forehead is toward the top of the figure. The first scan on the left is at the widest part of the brain (for example, nose level), and each successive scan slices through the brain moving up to the top of the head. The darkest shading corresponds to the number of patients with brain damage in the same location, and it can be seen that those with the most spiritual experiences had damage toward the front of the brain.

This result is consistent with Newberg's findings. The front of the brain is associated with executive functions, such as planning, working memory, inhibition, and abstract reasoning. Cristofori proposes that decreased functioning of the prefrontal cortex (in this case from bullet damage) is correlated with spiritual experiences. The researchers go beyond the data to propose that normal executive functioning inhibits spiritual experiences. This makes intuitive sense. During the practice of Buddhist meditation, monks inhibit their executive functions to clear their minds and allow "being," not "doing." This practice seems to allow the spiritual to arise.

Another famous example is the left hemisphere stroke experienced by neuroscientist Jill Bolte Taylor. A stroke would cause a decrease in brain activity in the affected region. Of this experience, she wrote, "And here, deep within the absence of earth temporality, the boundaries of my earthly body dissolved and I melted into the universe. . . . In the absence of my left hemisphere's analytical judgment, I was completely entranced by the feelings of tranquility, safety, blessedness, euphoria, and omniscience."[41]

While these new results are still being discussed, the remarkable suggestion here is that lowering activity in the front part of the brain can actually increase spiritual experiences. Damage in the brain due to dementia is not like stroke or bullet damage, but in principle there could be parallel effects.

Indeed, neurologist Bruce Miller found emergence of musical talent in some people with frontotemporal dementia that he attributes to damage in the left anterior temporal lobe areas. He writes, "Loss of function in one brain area can release new functions elsewhere."[42] We posit here that dementia does not categorically terminate spirituality, and it is not beyond the understanding of modern science that spirituality might increase.

Conclusion

Music, spirituality, the self, and humor are spread throughout the brain, and the diseases that cause dementia do not necessarily remove them. We cannot presume to know all the subtleties the person with dementia is experiencing. But concepts such as the "self," "consciousness," and "spirituality" that were previously conjectures by philosophers and theologians are now aspects that researchers are beginning to measure in the brain. There is much controversy, but the work of this chapter shows that the brain is far more complex than most of us imagined. We should not underestimate its abilities, even in the face of damage due to disease. Alzheimer's disease and related dementias are due to disease in an organ of the body, no more, no less. The stigma that surrounds them is not logical.

The brain is indeed an amazing phenomenon and is a wondrous part of creation, truly a sign of God's glory. Cognitive psychologist Steven Pinker expresses the views of many when he proposes that the human brain may ultimately be too limited for us to understand ourselves:

> The brain is a product of evolution, and just as animal brains have their limitations, we have ours. Our brains can't hold a hundred numbers in memory, can't visualize seven-dimensional space, and perhaps can't intuitively grasp why neural information processing observed from the outside should give rise to subjective experience on the inside. This is where I place my bet, though I admit that the theory could be demolished when an unborn genius—a Darwin or Einstein of consciousness—comes up with a flabbergasting new idea that suddenly makes it all clear to us.[43]

Psychologist and theologian J. Harold Ellens writes, "You could say that we live in a matrix of forces that looks natural and mundane but is in fact transcendental."[44] In the end we are left to marvel at the origin of the brain's orderliness, and how the beauty and complexity that is our brain is reflective of the greatness of the one Holy God.

Reflection Questions

✳ Does the recent discovery of the memory capacity of the healthy human brain change your view of human potential? Freud said that even before what we say is our first memory, our brains have stored a huge amount of previous experience. What is your earliest memory, and has the answer to this question changed over your adult life? Why do you think you chose this as your earliest memory? How might we honor the gift of memory?

✳ Do you think about keeping your brain healthy, as we have been taught to keep our hearts healthy? How do you take care of your mental health, cherish it, and appreciate it, as much as your physical health?

✳ When you pray, what do you pray with? Jesus said to love God "with all your heart, and with all your soul, and with all your mind" (Matt. 22:37). Back in the day, they believed the heart, rather than the brain, was the "thinking center." How does it feel to love God with all your brain, your soul, and your mind?

✳ We don't know if all spiritual experiences have a physical basis. The ones discussed in the Cristofori study seem to. Does it lessen spiritual experiences if it's true they have a physical basis? Are they totally generated by our intentions—by our consciously or subconsciously manipulating a part of our brain? What about the ones that we don't ask for, the ones that just come spontaneously, "without any warning or desire on our part" (as St. Teresa of Avila described)?

✳ If we broaden our thinking, can we conclude that in order to experience God spiritually, we need to surrender our strong egocentric tendencies to be in control? ("For we do not know how to pray as we ought, but that very Spirit intercedes with sighs too deep for words" [Rom. 8:26].)

Notes

1. Keith Ward, *By Faith and Reason: The Essential Keith Ward*, eds. Wm. Curtis Holtzen and Roberto Sirvent (Eugene, OR: Wipf and Stock, 2012). On p. 155, he writes, "the subject of consciousness is capable in principle of substantial existence, and therefore of continued existence in some other form of body."

2. John Polkinghorn, *Living with Hope* (Louisville, KY: Westminster John Knox Press, 2003). On p. 45 he writes,

> The real me is not the ever-changing atoms of my body, but it is the immensely complex, information-bearing pattern in which those atoms are organized. It is that pattern that is the soul, an idea that fits in with what twenty-first-century science is beginning to discover from the study of complex systems, that information is as fundamental a category as energy.

3. Wesley Wildman, "A Theological Challenge: Coordinating Biological, Social, and Religious Visions of Humanity," *Zygon* 33, no. 4 (1998): 571-597.
4. David Keck, *Forgetting Whose We Are* (Nashville: Abingdon Press, 1996), 13.
5. Jeannette Norden, *The Human Brain* (Chantilly, VA: The Teaching Company, 2007), 1.
6. Peggy Mason, *Medical Neurobiology*, 2nd ed. (New York: Oxford University Press, 2017), 6.
7. Michel Hofman, "Evolution of the Human Brain: When Bigger is Better," *Frontiers in Neuroanatomy* 8 (2014): 15.
8. Carl Zimmer, "The New Science of the Brain," *National Geographic Magazine*, February 2014, 36.
9. Image adapted from Ruopeng Wang, Lawrence L. Wald, Athinoula A. Martinos, *Science* 342, no. 6158 (2013): cover.
10. Carla Shatz, "The Developing Brain," *Scientific American* 267 (1992): 60-67, doi:10.1038/scientificamerican0992-60.
11. Thomas M. Bartol Jr., Cailey Bromer, Justin Kinney, et al., "Nanoconnectomic Upper Bound on the Variability of Synaptic Plasticity," *eLife* 4:e10778 (2015), doi: 10.7554/eLife.10778.
12. Candace Pert, Michael Ruff, Richard Weber, and Miles Herkenham, "Neuropeptides and their Receptors: A Psychosomatic Network," *Journal of Immunology* 135 (1985): 820-826.
13. Gregory of Nyssa, "On the Soul and Resurrection," quoted in Kathryn Tanner, *Christ the Key* (Cambridge: Cambridge University Press, 2010), 38.
14. Peter Eriksson et al., "Neurogenesis in the Adult Human Hippocampus," *Nature Medicine* 4 (1998): 1313-1317.
15. Kirk Erickson et al., "Exercise Training Increases Size of Hippocampus and Improves Memory," *Proceedings of the National Academy of Science* 108 (2011): 3017-3022.
16. R. Quian Quiroga, L. Reddy, G. Kreiman, et al., "Invariant Visual Representation by Single Neurons in the Human Brain," *Nature* 435 (2005): 1102-1107.

17. Clive G. Ballard et al., "Aromatherapy as a Safe and Effective Treatment for the Management of Agitation in Severe Dementia: the Results of a Double-blind, Placebo-controlled Trial with Melissa," *Journal of Clinical Psychiatry* 63, no. 7 (2002): 553-558.

18. D. P. Devanand et al., "Olfactory Deficits Predict Cognitive Decline and Alzheimer Dementia in an Urban Community," *Neurology* 84, no. 2 (2015): 182-189.

19. Luke Mastin, "The Human Memory," last modified 2010, accessed May 2, 2016, http://www.lukemastin.com/humanmemory/types.html.

20. Amee Baird and Séverine Samson, "Memory for Music in Alzheimer's Disease: Unforgettable?" *Neuropsychology Review* 19 (2009): 85-101.

21. Mason, 460.

22. Lulu Xie et al., "Sleep Drives Metabolite Clearance from the Adult Brain," *Science* 342, no. 6156 (2013): 373-377.

23. Alice Parker, interview by Krista Tippett, "Singing is the Most Companionable of Arts," *On Being*, National Public Radio, December 8, 2016, accessed November 11, 2017, https://onbeing.org/programs/alice-parker-singing-is-the -most-companionable-of-arts.

24. "Man in Nursing Home Reacts to Hearing Music from His Era," musicandmemory .org, accessed November 6, 2017, https://www.youtube.com/watch?v=fyZQ f0p73QM.

25. Naomi Feil, "Gladys Wilson and Naomi Feil," accessed November 18, 2017, https://www.youtube.com/watch?v=CrZXz10FcVM.

26. Jörn-Henrik Jacobsen et al., "Why Musical Memory can be Preserved in Advanced Alzheimer's Disease," *Brain* 138 (2015): 2438-2450.

27. Michael Glasser et al., "A Multi-modal Parcellation of Human Cerebral Cortex," *Nature* 536 (2016): 171-178.

28. Jacobsen et al., 2438-2450.

29. Editorial, "In Search of Self," *Nature Neuroscience* 5 (2002): 1099.

30. Norden, 13.

31. Jia Liu, Alison Harris, and Nancy Kanwisher, "Perception of Face Parts and Face Configurations: An fMRI Study," *Journal of Cognitive Neuroscience* 22, no. 1 (2010): 203–211.

32. Norden, 24.

33. Christof Koch et al., reported in "Giant Neuron Encircles Entire Brain of a Mouse," by Sara Reardon, *Nature* 543 (2017): 14-15.

34. Norden, 25.

35. Andrew Newberg et al., "The Measurement of Regional Cerebral Blood Flow during the Complex Cognitive Task of Meditation: a Preliminary SPECT Study," *Psychiatry Research: Neuroimaging* 106, no. 2 (2001): 113-122.

36. Andrew Newberg and Mark Robert Waldman, *How Enlightenment Changes Your Brain* (New York: Avery, 2017), 86.

37. Ibid., 91.

38. Irene Cristofori, Joseph Bulbulia, John H. Shaver, et al., "Neural Correlates of Mystical Experience," *Neurophysologia* 80 (2016): 212-220.

39. Frederick S. Barrett, Matthew W. Johnson, and Roland R. Griffiths, "Validation of the Revised Mystical Experience Questionnaire in Experimental Sessions with Psilocybin," *Journal of Psychopharmacology* 29, no. 11 (2015): 1182-1190.

40. Cristofori, 216.

41. Jill Bolte Taylor, *My Stroke of Insight: A Brain Scientist's Personal Journey* (New York: Viking, 2009), 50-51.

42. B. L. Miller, K. Boone, J. L. Cummings, et al., "Functional Correlates of Musical and Visual Ability in Fronto-temporal Dementia," *British Journal of Psychiatry* 176 (2000): 458-463, doi: 10.1192/bjp.176.5.458.

43. Steven Pinker, "The Brain. The Mystery of Consciousness," *Time Magazine*, January 29, 2007, accessed November 18, 2017, http://content.time.com/time/magazine/article/0,9171,1580394-6,00.html.

44. J. Harold Ellens, *Understanding Religious Experiences: What the Bible Says about Spirituality* (Westport, CT: Praeger, 2008), 96.

CHAPTER 2

The Brain Affected by Dementia

Dementia is a progressive brain deterioration, including loss of memory, judgment, language, complex motor skills, and other intellectual functions caused by the permanent damage or death of the brain's neurons. At other times in history, various diseases were largely responsible for most dementia. In 1900, only about 4 percent of the population was over age sixty-five, and the most prominent cause of dementia was long-term syphilis. Now that people are living longer—in the United States, 15 percent of the population is now over age sixty-five—Alzheimer's disease is the most common cause of dementia. It is responsible for 60 to 80 percent of dementia cases and is the sixth leading cause of death. Other diseases causing dementia include Lewy Body disease, vascular dementia, frontotemporal dementia, stroke, Huntington's, Parkinson's, Creutzfeldt Jacob, alcoholism, and AIDS. Because it is so prominent, we will focus on Alzheimer's disease in this chapter. Observations in the following chapters about the spirituality and acceptance of those with dementia are applicable to all diseases causing dementia.

It is important to distinguish dementia from other forms of memory loss associated with aging, which are often a normal part of growing older. This is at least in part because blood flow, sleep, repair mechanisms, and other factors are less efficient as a person ages. The memory-related structure in the center of the brain called the hippocampus loses 5 percent of its cells every decade due to normal aging, starting around age twenty-five. Normal aging might include forgetting names or appointments but remembering them later, sometimes having trouble finding the right word, and misplacing objects like house keys, then retracing steps and finding them later.

In between Alzheimer's and normal aging is a condition called mild cognitive impairment (MCI)—problems with memory, language, thinking, and judgment. People with this condition may be aware that their memory or mental function has "slipped," and others may notice too. These slips are not severe enough to significantly interfere with their day-to-day activities. Examples include forgetting appointments or social events, losing a train of thought or the thread of the conversation, feeling overwhelmed by making decisions or interpreting instructions, having trouble finding their way around familiar environments, and becoming more impulsive or showing poor judgment. Many people over age sixty-five have MCI; some may go on to develop Alzheimer's, but many do not. In some individuals, the condition reverses or remains stable.

Scientifically, the illnesses that cause dementia are illnesses of the brain, no more and no less. Just as we do not stigmatize other illnesses, such as those of the heart or other organs, there are no valid reasons to stigmatize dementia.

Agent of Alzheimer's Disease

Alzheimer's disease is a degenerative disease causing deterioration of brain functions over a period of five to twenty years (average of eight).[1] The healthy brain has mechanisms for clearing out metabolites and toxins that build up as a result of use. As mentioned in chapter 1, researchers have suggested that much of this important "cleaning" function occurs during sleep. Beta-amyloid is a small protein that forms naturally in the brain. Its normal role is not yet understood but some think at normal levels it serves a protective function. The "amyloid hypothesis" held by some researchers argues that beta-amyloid protein builds up in toxic levels and coagulates into a plaque, a microscopic grayish-white substance, in areas *outside* the brain cells. Up until recently, plaque could only be observed during an autopsy. Now plaque buildup can be seen in a living person during a PET scan. Other scans, such as CAT, SPECT, and various forms of MRI, can reveal other signs of Alzheimer's, including brain atrophy.

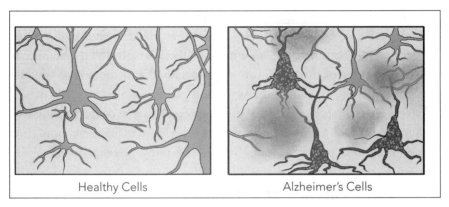

Healthy Cells	Alzheimer's Cells

The view under a microscope of healthy neurons (left) versus those in Alzheimer's (right), which shows grayish-white balls of plaque outside the brain cells and dark-colored tangles of tau protein inside the triangular cell bodies.

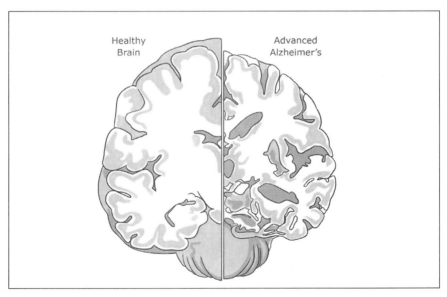

A view of the brain during autopsy: the left shows a healthy brain with intact outer folds of the cerebral cortex, and the right shows a brain with advanced Alzheimer's, with shrinkage due to neuronal death and an increased size of ventricles (open spaces in the brain that contain fluids).

Additionally, tau proteins, also normally found in the brain, can build up to form dark-colored fibrous tangles *inside* the brain cells. During the course of Alzheimer's disease, excess plaque and tangles eventually kill the brain cells, causing shrinkage of the brain. It is not understood why the plaque and tangles grow unchecked, which means the real cause of Alzheimer's has not yet been discovered. It is not known if the plaque and tangles cause the illness, or if they are a byproduct of the disease. Does the brain make these proteins to protect itself from the real cause? The answer is not yet clear.

Stages of Dementia and Retention

In discussing Alzheimer's disease, experts have found it important not only to acknowledge the losses, but also to emphasize what *remains* at each stage, which, given the complexity of the human brain as described in chapter 1, is significant. The first area affected by the plaque and tangles is the hippocampus, that part of the brain thought to be responsible for consolidation of short-term memory to long-term memory and organization of spatial information. The decreased functionality of the hippocampus results in short-term memory loss and disorientation that are usually the first symptoms of Alzheimer's. As the plaques and tangles accumulate in other areas, other symptoms develop in a roughly predictable pattern through early, middle, and late stages of the illness.[2] It is *not* true that the entire brain becomes damaged. A widely circulated Facebook post about Alzheimer's incorrectly describes the process as, "Imprisoned in one's own rapidly shrinking brain is how a doctor described it to me."[3] This kind of misinformation only elevates the stigma and fear of dementia.

Alzheimer's disease occurs in three stages. The early stage is characterized by loss of day-to-day memory and difficulty executing tasks, such as balancing a checkbook or using the phone. Memory, thinking, and planning are some of the first functions affected. There is anecdotal repetition and spatial disorientation as a result of declining place recognition and navigation skills. There may be a desire to "go home," even if one is at home. Sundowning is the phenomenon of increased irritability, agitation, and even hallucinations that occur as the sun is setting. Its origin is not known exactly, but researchers measured increased levels of the stress hormone cortisol around this time of day in some people with dementia, which might cause sundowning.[4]

In the early stages of Alzheimer's, decision-making associated with the executive function area of the brain also becomes impaired, making driving a car and handling money difficult. Episodic memory is affected, characterized by people forgetting recently learned information, asking for the same information over and over, losing track of seasons and dates, and forgetting where they are and how they got there. It can be difficult for people with dementia to recognize objects and what they are used for (agnosia). They might put objects in unusual places, such as placing keys in a freezer. They may also have difficulty recognizing people and experience personality changes and fluctuations in mood. Pastoral concerns at this stage include the intense grief and anxiety of both the person developing dementia and their loved ones. It is especially important to encourage them to find spiritual and social support, as discussed in chapter 7.

A great deal of brain activity remains in the early stage to support most daily functions. Most (80 percent) people in this stage are often still at home, with caregiving provided by family or in-home services. Many choose assisted living facilities, which often simulate a person's home since use of their own furnishings is typically permitted. People still recognize and enjoy family and friends and attend religious services. Traditions can still be honored at holidays, and dinners out or other events can still be enjoyed. It is a time for family reunions, enjoying children, pets, and beloved hobbies. Some professionals in the field have noted that on occasion, people can "blossom" in the early stages as they leave behind burdens that were weighing them down in the past.

The drawing of a brain slice in the figure on the next page corresponding to the early stage shows the tau protein damage in the brain (dark shading) starting near the hippocampus.[5]

In the middle stage, shown on page 31, a person will increasingly use his or her long-term memory. People may think, for example, that they are back in their childhood home.

* * *

When my mother began to forget who I was, she thought I was her best friend from high school. While I was of course upset by the progression of her illness, I came to admire this adaptation by my mother,

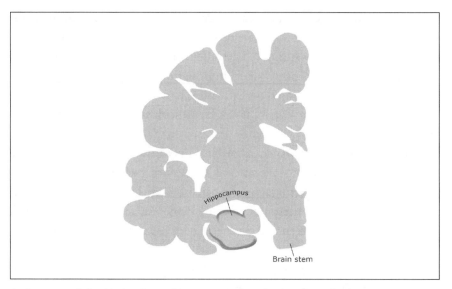

A drawing of the brain slice of a person who died with early dementia, showing the damage to the hippocampal region by the tau proteins.

> because she was drawing on her long-term memory and shifting as best she could, putting me in a category of a loved one. My first inclination was to try to correct her, but I found it worked best if we stayed in this alternate reality, which only lasted a little while. I cherished the thought of being mom's best friend and reflected on how we could be in different roles but still share love.—*Janice*

✳ ✳ ✳

Other challenges surface in the middle stage. Language difficulties result from damage to the language parts of the brain. Aphasia is the difficulty or loss of ability to speak or understand words and the involuntary repetition of words. People in the middle stage of Alzheimer's begin to have difficulty forming sentences. There are challenges associated with travel as the person loses physical coordination, has difficulty walking, and perhaps develops incontinence. A person's behavior may be aggressive, paranoid, or impulsive. In the past decade, a great deal has been learned about behavioral changes. There are many aspects of a person's living conditions to check before assuming that the behaviors are not borne out of physical or emotional discomfort.[6]

The role of the person providing pastoral care during this stage can be a ministry of presence, assuring the person with dementia that he or she is unseparated from God's love and still part of the community (they will not be alone). Theologian John Swinton encourages giving people with dementia "the benefit of the doubt."[7] Short pieces of familiar scripture and hymns are likely to help connect with a person through his or her religious history, as well as symbols such as candles, a cross, rosary, or book of Holy Scripture. Caregivers and family may need support with difficult decisions concerning increased nursing needs and a possible move to a care facility. Social workers can also be of enormous help with complex decisions, including financial ones.

People with dementia in the middle stage might still be at home with full-time caregiving, or in an assisted living facility. They sometimes recognize loved ones and enjoy reminiscing cued by old photos and beloved objects from their past, such as a Memory Box, as discussed in chapter 6. They may still enjoy food, although finger food usually works best as managing cutlery becomes difficult. Socializing, singing, and reciting scripture may be appropriate. Conversations are possible if caregivers and guests maintain a slower but normal rhythm of dialogue and provide most of the narrative. Using familiar idioms, such as "good to the last drop," or even family jokes can often

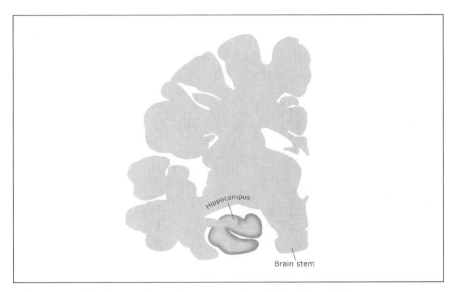

A drawing of the brain slice of a person who died with middle-stage dementia, showing further damage to the hippocampus by the tau proteins.[8]

bring laughter and comfort. This stage has its challenges but it is not without moments of joy, laughter, and spirituality.

The late stage shown below is characterized by a pronounced decline in cognition and the inability of the person with dementia to communicate or care for themselves. Usually there is a great amount of time spent sleeping or dozing, even if the person is sitting up or in a wheelchair. The person may need to be fed, and depending on dental conditions and how well she is swallowing, she may require pureed foods. Health wise, she may encounter more frequent infections, such as urinary tract infections that are quite common and can cause mental as well as physical malaise. Untreated, these infections can lead to sepsis and even death. Pneumonia is also a risk, often due to food or drink going into the windpipe ("aspirating") and causing infection. Treating infections and other medical issues may present challenges to the family.[9] Dementia-specific advanced medical directives that lay out goals of care at various stages of dementia are very helpful. Having a healthcare power of attorney, durable power of attorney, and funds in a joint checking account are very important.

Ultimately in the final stage of the illness, the body begins to shut down, presumably as the brain becomes less capable of supporting it. The process

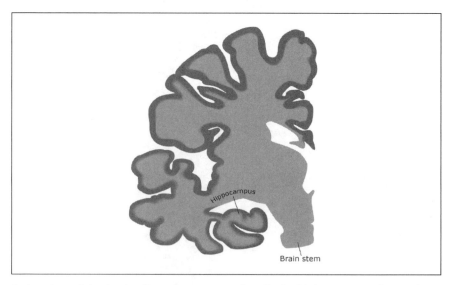

A drawing of the brain slice of a person who died with late-stage dementia, showing extensive damage to the hippocampus and the cerebral cortex.[10]

may begin with the person not wanting as much food or rejecting even favorite foods. Medical and hospice staff are quick to educate the family that the person is not intentionally starving themselves; rather, the body is rejecting food because there is no need or energy for it. Forcing food at this time can cause the person great physical discomfort. Requirements in different states vary, but hospice care may be appropriate. During this time, pastoral needs are centered on spiritual comfort and assurance for the person with dementia and the family. It is a time for family and friends to express their love and gratitude. Familiar music and prayers are treasured aspects of the end-of-life ritual. The dying process can be quite peaceful.

In the final stage of a disease like Alzheimer's, love and spirituality, as well as the enjoyment of touch and music, seem to still be present. There may be occasional coherent sentences that carry a great deal of meaning and are well worth the patience of waiting. Swinton calls these "sporadic lucidity."[11] Some report that people who are dying have moments of lucidity, knowing death is near. As an old hymn says, "And the things of Earth will grow strangely dim in the light of His glory and grace."[12] We don't know the experiences those with late-stage dementia are having. It is a privilege to accompany them during a very sacred time.

In the progression of Alzheimer's disease, there is a great deal of loss, similar to an ascetic's journey—a winnowing of everything else to leave the truths of love and spirituality, the comfort of touch, and the appreciation of music. While science has much to say about the losses associated with short- and long-term memory, physical coordination, executive and even primitive functions, it does not seem to explain the important aspects that remain. In the end, the "truths" seem to be all that have meaning and that matter.

Diagnosing Alzheimer's Disease

Alzheimer's disease is related to aging, but it is *not* normal aging. Many try to normalize dementia in elders by accepting it as a part of aging. It should be seen, however, as a disease like any other that needs a diagnosis and treatment. There are important reasons why diagnosing dementia is essential. First, memory loss could be due to a different physical problem, such as an infection. It is important to get an accurate diagnosis because treatment may be available. Other possible causes of memory loss include complications from medications, brain tumors or stroke, Parkinson's, depression, B12 deficiency, and thyroid disease. Secondly, it is important to know the diagnosis to begin planning for care, identifying caregivers, and finding an appropriate residence. A specialist, such as a neurologist or geriatrician, is recommended because of the complexity of the diagnosis. Testing includes laboratory analysis, brain-imaging, and neuropsychological examinations. Support groups can help both the person with dementia as well as the family learn about resources in the area and obtain advice for maximizing quality of life.

Risks of Alzheimer's

The greatest risk for Alzheimer's disease is age. In the United States, 3 percent of people ages sixty-five to seventy-four have Alzheimer's, 17 percent of those seventy-five to eighty-four, and 32 percent of people eighty-five or older. Of all the people who have Alzheimer's disease, 82 percent are age seventy-five or older. While there is always hope for a cure, this rate might triple by 2050 because of the increased number of elderly in the United States.

Two-thirds of those with Alzheimer's are women. The reason for this is not known but factors could be women tend to live longer, the possible connection of the disease to estrogen levels, and lower educational attainment for the current generation. African Americans are roughly twice as likely as Caucasians to have Alzheimer's, and among Latinos the factor is one and a half times as likely. Incidence of Alzheimer's is lowest for Asian Americans. The racial differences may be related to the incidence of cardiovascular disease and diabetes among racial groups. Some evidence points to differences in socioeconomic risk factors, such as early life adversity and discrimination, poverty, lower educational attainment, and healthcare disparities.[13] Education has been associated with a modest slowing of the Alzheimer's disease rate lately, emphasizing the concept of "cognitive reserve"—that is, the more the brain is used and synapses are formed, the better the resilience toward dementia later in life.[14]

The origin of Alzheimer's is not known, but many believe it is caused by multiple factors. The only truly inherited type occurs in a very small number of cases (under 1 percent) and usually results in an early onset before age sixty-five. This is called "familial Alzheimer's disease." In addition, three-quarters of people over age sixty-five with Down syndrome (a genetic disorder) get Alzheimer's disease.

Family history and the occurrence of a gene called APOE4 increase risk but do not always result in Alzheimer's. There are three types of the APOE gene: APOE2, E3, and E4. Everyone has two copies of the APOE gene, which means, for example, a person may be E2/E2 or E2/E3, and so on. The most common type is E3, and it carries no risk for Alzheimer's. Having E2 is somewhat rare and appears to reduce risk. The E4 gene apparently puts people at risk for Alzheimer's. Having one copy of E4 (for example, E3/E4) can increase risk by two to three times (about 20 percent of the population is expected to have this combination). Having two copies (E4/E4) can increase the risk by twelve times (only 3 percent of the population has E4/E4). It is estimated that 40 to 65 percent of people with Alzheimer's have one to two copies of the E4 version of the gene. One copy of APOE comes from each of one's parents. If a parent has Alzheimer's, the parent could have zero, one, or two copies of APOE4, and if one, it does not necessarily follow that he or she will pass that gene on. Testing for the gene is not ordinarily done outside of clinical trials. While the test is available to the public through direct-to-consumer companies, it is important to be prepared psychologically and realize that there is no consensus on how to prevent dementia in each of the genetic cases.

Additional risks include a history of traumatic brain injury, such as falls, car accidents, or sports injuries. Some risks for Alzheimer's can be modified. We already mentioned the value of aerobic exercise, which is universally agreed to be beneficial for everyone. Some studies describe "aerobic exercise" as twenty minutes in duration, three to five times per week, with breathing at an intensity that makes it difficult to carry on a conversation. Exercise serves to build up the cardio-vascular system, including the small capillaries in the brain that are important in delivering nutrients, removing toxins and harmful metabolites, and preventing small brain bleeds or strokes. As discussed in chapter 1, exercise can also increase the growth factor, BDNF, which encourages growth of new neurons in the hippocampus.

Diet also seems to be extremely important. "Good" fat found in walnuts, avocados, olives, salmon, and other foods are preferred fuels for the brain over sugar or "bad" fat. Lean proteins, vegetables, low amounts of sugar and carbohydrates, and adequate hydration are all considered healthy eating for the brain. Some of these diet practices may result in a healthier gut microbiome, tied by some to brain health. It is important to manage cardiovascular risk factors (diabetes, obesity, smoking, and hypertension), which also can harm the brain. Good sleep habits and management of stress and depression are also important. Social and cognitive engagement are important, along with learning new skills such as a second language or playing a musical instrument. Managing these factors does not guarantee that people will not get Alzheimer's—and may only delay it—but one study estimates Alzheimer's cases worldwide could be reduced by one-third if these factors were controlled.[15]

Maintaining good health habits to prevent amyloid plaque buildup is important as early as middle age. The plaques are observed in the brain as much as a decade before diagnosis of Alzheimer's disease.[16]

Hope

While there is as yet no cure for Alzheimer's, there is hope in new understandings of the brain and the origin of Alzheimer's, its diagnosis, and in how to care for those with dementia. Several promising drug trials are getting underway. At present the only drugs available (for example, Aricept and Namenda) work with neurotransmitters in the brain, as discussed in chapter 1. The drugs temporarily slow the progress of the illness and/or slightly improve symptoms. These drug interventions are not very effective past the middle stage of Alzheimer's. The ability to do brain imaging to detect early signs of Alzheimer's is promising because it is easier to treat healthier brains. Scientists say that it is much harder to repair damage once it has been done.

Thomas Aquinas wrote, "Faith has to do with things that are not seen and hope with things that are not at hand." We are called to pray for a cure for dementia and to support research to better understand and prevent the diseases that cause it. We can pass on that hope through our acceptance of and love for people with dementia.

Reflection Questions

✳ How do you describe dementia? If dementia is a symptom of a disease, why do we treat it differently than other diseases, such as cancer?

✳ How could you counter misinformation about dementia? How does knowledge about dementia begin to redeem it from the stigma and fear associated with it?

✳ How could you provide a ministry of presence for someone who has dementia?

✳ What physical practices do you already do to lower the risk of Alzheimer's? What additional practices could you add?

✳ David Keck writes, "We all have faulty memories, we all become incoherent at times, we all need caregiving."[17] Is our discomfort with dementia partially due to fears of our own shortcomings? How might these fears affect our caregiving?

✳ How important is memory to your faith? Knowing how Alzheimer's disease disrupts memories, what do you think would happen to faith?

Notes

1. "What is Alzheimer's?" Alzheimer's Association, last modified 2018, accessed March 16, 2018, http://www.alz.org/alzheimers_disease_what_is_alzheimers.asp.

2. David Sweatt, *Mechanisms of Memory* (Amsterdam: Elsevier, 2010), 296.

3. Forums: Dementia-related News and Campaigns, Alzheimer's Society, accessed April 15, 2017, https://forum.alzheimers.org.uk/showthread.php?92887-Inaccurate-rubbish.

4. Massimo Venturelli et al., "Effectiveness of Exercise- and Cognitive-Based Treatments on Salivary Cortisol Levels and Sundowning Syndrome Symptoms in Patients with Alzheimer's Disease," *Journal of Alzheimer's Disease* 53, no. 4 (2016): 1631-1640.

5. Sweatt, 296.

6. "Behavioral Symptoms," Alzheimer's Association, accessed March 11, 2018, https://www.alz.org/professionals_and_researchers_behavioral_symptoms_pr.asp.

7. John Swinton, *Dementia: Living in the Memories of God* (Grand Rapids, MI: William B. Eerdmans Publishing Company, 2012), 59.

8. Sweatt, 296.

9. Hank Dunn, *Hard Choices for Loving People: CPR, Artificial Feeding, Comfort Care and the Patient with a Life-Threatening Illness* (Leesburg, VA: A&A Publishers, 2009).

10. Sweatt, 296.

11. Swinton, 243.

12. "Turn Your Eyes Upon Jesus," Helen H. Lemmel, 1922.

13. Fredrick Kunkle, "Stress of Poverty, Racism Raise Risk of Alzheimer's for African Americans, New Research Suggests," *Washington Post*, July 16, 2017, accessed December 27, 2017, https://www.washingtonpost.com/local/social-issues/stress -of-poverty-and-racism-raise-risk-of-alzheimers-for-african-americans-new -research-suggests/2017/07/15/4a16e918-68c9-11e7-a1d7-9a32c91c6f40 _story.html?utm_term=.dbefdc26a6a4.

14. Yu-Tzu Wu et al., "The Changing Prevalence and Incidence of Dementia over Time—Current Evidence," *Nature Reviews Neurology* 13, no. 6 (2017): 327-339, doi: 10.1038/nrneurol.2017.63.

15. Sam Norton et al., "Potential for Primary Prevention of Alzheimer's Disease: An Analysis of Population-Based Data," *Lancet Neurology* 13, no. 8 (2014): 788-794, doi: 10.1016/S1474-4422(14)70136-X.

16. Reisa A. Sperling et al., "Toward Defining the Preclinical Stages of Alzheimer's Disease: Recommendations from The National Institute on Aging and the Alzheimer's Association Workgroup," *Alzheimer's and Dementia* 7, no. 3 (2011): 280-292.

17. David Keck, *Forgetting Whose We Are* (Nashville: Abingdon Press, 1996), 16.

CHAPTER 3

Theology of the Human Person

In chapters 1 and 2, we took a scientific approach, describing human beings from the point of view of their physiology, especially the human brain when it is healthy versus when it is subject to Alzheimer's disease. Neuroscience is rapidly advancing but reaches its limits when describing all the phenomena associated with dementia. Here we turn to a theological approach, starting first with a theological description of the human being.

To fully describe people and their relationship to God is daunting, although theologians of each generation still make the attempt. Many of today's theologians take into account the considerable advances in scientific knowledge about humans. In chapter 1, we noted that no part of the human brain is known to be specifically dedicated to the "self," with the "sense of the self" instead distributed in different parts of the brain and possibly beyond. In fact, science has difficulty explaining why we experience a sense of self and how that is defined. We also noted that dementia has been called the "theological disease" because it calls into question exactly what makes us human.

Historically, the concept of *rationality* was central in explaining how people differ from other higher animals. Early theologians believed God communicates with us through our rationality. But this single criterion is inadequate, especially when applied to people with dementia. We live in what bioethicist

Stephen Post calls a "hypercognitive" culture that overvalues rationality.[1] When people develop dementia, are they less of a person? Do they lose their connection to God? Some say yes, but in this chapter and the next, we argue strongly against such a conclusion. Conscious or not, such beliefs can create harmful scenarios for people with dementia. Seeing a person as "less than" raises a general fear of these labels and categories, ultimately degrading the care for the person with dementia, which degrades us all.

What does the Church say about the nature of the self and being a person? This question falls within the subdiscipline of theological anthropology, or reflections on what it means to be human, which is a central topic theologians face in articulating Christian faith. What we need is theology that has a more balanced view of our relationship with God and each other. It is not just rationality that makes us human or intellect that draws us closer to God.

The focus of this chapter on theology is based on the work of contemporary theologian David Kelsey, due to the clarity of his thought on this issue. His recent book, *Eccentric Existence*, integrates knowledge from many disciplines: theology, anthropology, religion, psychology, ethics, and science. The title comes from his central belief that we are human because God relates to us. The basis for the value and relationship of the human being lies in God; it comes from outside the human beings themselves. God is in the center, and people are outside the center, or ex-centric (*eccentric*).

Historical Concepts

It is helpful to understand the ancient Greek concept of soul and the Judeo-Christian doctrine of Imago Dei, because both have influenced the Western understanding of the human person.

The meaning of "soul" in ancient Athens stemmed from Plato's concepts in *The Republic* (book IV) and *Phaedrus*. Plato muses about the soul having three principles: the rational, the irrational associated with desire, and the passionate associated with courage, as in military heroism.[2] He writes, "ought not the rational principle, which is wise, and has the care of the whole soul, to rule, and the passionate or spirited principle to be the subject and ally?"[3] Plato used a metaphor of a charioteer (rationality) driving two winged horses (the other two principles). To Plato, all three principles contribute to harmony and are needed to ascend to heaven.

While the Bible does not offer a definitive explanation of what it means to be human, one of the most enduring Judeo-Christian concepts comes from the creation story in the book of Genesis:

> Then God said, "Let us make humankind in our image, according to our likeness; and let them have dominion over the fish of the sea, and over the birds of the air, and over the cattle, and over all the wild animals of the earth, and over every creeping thing that creeps upon the earth." So God created humankind in his image, in the image of God he created them; male and female he created them. (Gen. 1:26–27)

The Hebrew words for image (*selem*) and likeness (*demuth*) are understood to mean "similar to but not the same as" God. The doctrine labeled "Imago Dei," Latin for "image of God," signifies the special status that humans have in creation, since according to Genesis no other species enjoys the distinction of being made in God's image.

Many current biblical scholars believe that the term "image of God" (*selem 'elohim*) was taken from Neo-Assyrian and Neo-Babylonian cultures, which held that kings were representatives of the gods and made in the image of the gods.[4] The use of this phrase attempts to express that God made all of humanity as God's royal representatives on earth. The argument is made more compelling by the juxtaposition of the text "and let them have dominion." This modern scholarship on the phrase "image of God" sheds new meaning compared to the historical interpretations of Imago Dei, which tended to be more literal.

While modern interpretations of Imago Dei may challenge the historical, the latter continue to influence Western thought today. Many of the early Church Fathers (300 to 600 CE) linked the Imago Dei in humans to the mind/spirit or soul, which is ranked higher than the body. The body cannot have the image of God, because God is immaterial and has no body, they reasoned. For Basil the Great, the "I" is the inner, the rational aspect of the human. He writes, "the outer things are not me but mine. . . . For I am not the hand, but I am the rational part of the soul. And the hand is a limb of the human being. Therefore, the body is an instrument of the human being, an instrument of the soul, and the human being is principally the soul in itself."[5] Basil goes so far as to say that only the rational part is the human being.

Augustine generally espouses that the soul is the core of the human being, and continues after bodily death. In *The Confessions*, he writes, " 'Who are you?' And I answered my own question: 'a man.' See, here are the body and soul that make up myself, the one outward and the other inward."[6] In *The Trinity*, he says the mind is one thing, but has two functions—the higher part contemplates eternal truths and makes judgments.[7] This "higher part" is in the image of God, and God communicates with us through it.

Just prior to the Enlightenment, René Descartes in *The Discourse on Method* describes sitting still with only his mind and his five senses. He attempted "to accept in them nothing more than what was presented to my mind so clearly and distinctly that I could have no occasion to doubt it."[8] His five senses, memories, and abstract thinking could deceive him, and so he doubts them. He comes to rely on the fact that *he is the one who is thinking* and concludes, "I think therefore I am." The rational part—thinking—defines the human person for Descartes. Western tradition that had already elevated the mind over the body embraced Descartes, and the rational became even more superior and the body more animalistic and undervalued, nothing more than a hydraulic machine. Descartes marries the soul with the mind. He writes, "For I consider the mind not part of the soul but as the whole of that soul which thinks."[9] The separation of mind and body became known as dualism.

Rationality as the main criterion of personhood continued throughout the Enlightenment in the eighteenth century and was strengthened with the Scientific Revolution. Today there still are dualists, but more recently evolved interpretations assume a united view of human nature.

From the Twentieth Century to Today

Twentieth-century theologian Karl Barth describes the human as "soul and body totally and simultaneously, in indissoluble differentiation, inseparable unity and indestructible order."[10] Barth does not mean the Augustinian idea of soul; rather, for him, the soul cannot exist without the body.

For Barth, to be human means to be in relationship with others. This comes from the concept of the Trinity; God's relationship within the Trinity is mirrored in humans in relationship with each other.[11] Barth explicitly rejects that the Imago Dei is the human's capacity for rational thought. He disagrees with the previous theologians who pursued "arbitrarily invented" interpretations of the Imago Dei that were too tied to their attempts to match God and human literally.[12]

A central idea in Barth's theology is that God seeks us more than we seek God, a concept he calls "the overflow":

> God is He who, without having to do so, seeks and creates fellowship between Himself and us. He does not have to do it, because in Himself without us, and therefore without this, He has that which He seeks and creates between Himself and us. We must certainly regard this overflow as itself matching His essence, belonging to his essence. But it is an overflow which is not demanded or presupposed by any necessity, constraint, or obligation, least of all from outside, from our side, or by any law by which God Himself is bound and obliged.[13]

Trying to imagine the bounty that Barth describes as the overflow is a deep mystery of our faith.

God recognizing us as a person, therefore, depends less upon our own particular state, since God seeks and creates fellowship with us. Our tie with God does not depend entirely on our own selves and minds, as Western individualistic culture is prone to think, but instead on the "overflow" of God's reach to us. This is especially comforting in the case of dementia because even if we forget God and our faith, we are assured that God will still reach for us.

Barth writes that it is not possible for humans to lose their one-ness, the unity that is soul and body—what one might call personhood but he calls "constitution." It is not touched by illness or death, and is only disturbed by—but not destroyed by—human sin:

> Since his constitution derives from this God, from Him who is faithful and does not repent of His goodness, it is therefore unshakeable. It can, of course, be disturbed and perverted by human sin, but it cannot be destroyed or rendered nugatory [of no value]. Hence man remains man even in his deepest fall, even in the last judgment of death; and even in death he is still man within the hand and power of God. . . . for man cannot be what he is, soul and body in ordered unity, without representing in himself—long before he understands it, and even when he will not understand it—the good intention of God towards him, without himself being guarantor for this good intention of God.[14]

Nancey Murphy, a contemporary theologian, attempts to bridge the modern scientific view of humans (described in chapter 1) with the Christian theological tradition. In *Bodies and Souls? Or Spirited Bodies?* she points out the success of modern neuroscience in explaining bodily and mental phenomena without referring to the immaterial.[15] The human, she believes, is composed of only one part (the body). The mind is constituted of electro-chemical signals generated in the brain and nervous system, involving movement of molecules and electrically charged ions in the body. Murphy writes, "all of the human capacities once attributed to the mind or soul are now being fruitfully studied as brain processes—or, more accurately, I should say, processes involving the brain, the rest of the nervous systems and other bodily systems, all interacting with the socio-cultural world."[16]

Some criticize Murphy's position as split (physicalism and theism) with no coherent linkage.[17] Steven Pinker (see his quote on page 20) might argue that we are inherently inadequate to understand the linkage (at least right now).

Murphy warns against seeing people only as physical organisms made of atoms that behave according to physical laws. She believes that all the functions previously attributed to the soul, including free will and moral responsibility, "depend on the body *in its relation to the world, to culture and to God.*"[18] We are "imbued with the legacy of thousands of years of culture, and most importantly, blown by the Breath of God's Spirit; we are *Spirited bodies.*"[19] We are distinct from animals, she writes, in morality and the ability to be in relationship with God. We have the capacity for religious experiences by virtue of culture and our complex neural systems (both given to us by God). Our identity is preserved over time through "consciousness, memory, moral character, interpersonal relationships, and especially our relationship with God."[20]

A consequence of Christians assuming the soul/body dualism for almost two millennia, says Murphy, is the emphasis on the individual as an isolated unit, the self (soul, mind, ego) that is contained in the body. When a person is viewed as an individual (which our culture tends to do), one's value is reduced by one's illness. But, Murphy notes, if a person is viewed as part of the household, as in the original Hebrew tradition, he maintains his standing in the psychological whole.[21]

Summary of Historical Overview

To summarize, the concept of soul that was embedded in ancient Greek thought through the ideas of Plato caught hold in Christianity through the work of the early Church fathers. Soul became associated with rationality and was elevated over the body. Several Church fathers equated soul with mind, but Descartes firmly separated mind from body in the teaching of dualism. To Basil, the body was an instrument of the soul, while to Descartes, the body was a hydraulic machine. The Enlightenment proclaimed rationality as the defining concept of being human.

Secular scientists and philosophers today argue that humans have one part—their body—that is governed only by physical laws. To them, people are "nothing but" atoms and simple materials, a product of ongoing processes regulated by natural laws and open to chance, albeit with highly complex brains. This view privileges rationality along with other cognitive functions such as language as the defining concepts separating humans from higher animals.

Similarly, interpretations of the Judeo-Christian concept of Imago Dei from Basil to Augustine elevated the rational because the image of God that humans reflected was attributed to intellect or soul.

More recent theology by Barth and Murphy anticipates a more balanced view with more fruitful outcomes, such as for the case of dementia. Barth's view of the Imago Dei links it to the covenant partnership between God and humans, not to particular human capacities like rationality. Barth views the human being as "soul and body in ordered unity," differing from Augustine's idea that body and soul are separate. Murphy goes one step further, claiming that humans have only a material body and no soul, with those aspects previously attributed to the soul emerging from a complex nervous system. Yet what is special about humans, she says, is that they have morality and can be in relationship with God.

Eccentric Existence

Christian theological anthropology is rooted in Genesis, which is the beginning of the one, long story of the Bible that ends in Revelation: creation, humanity's fall from grace, deliverance by God, and reunification at the end of the world. David Kelsey points out that many biblical scholars now believe that Genesis 1–2 are primeval history very much based on preexisting traditions from other cultures, for example, the Sumerians, about the origins of the world. Following other theologians, he recounts that in Genesis the stories are "bent" to serve as an introduction to the redemption story: God's call to Abraham and the deliverance of God's people at the Red Sea in Genesis 12–50. The first eleven chapters in Genesis, notes Kelsey, are like a "preface" to that story.[22]

Kelsey opines that grounding our view of human beings in Genesis 1 and 2 results in undesirable implications. The theologies that do so result in claims that some particular human capacity is the Image of God, and that "humans were created in a state of original righteousness and have 'fallen' from this prior state so that the image of God is damaged, obscured or destroyed."[23] What Kelsey finds disagreeable with this story is that individuals, rather than God, are at the center (anthropocentric). He also disagrees with the implications that death is unnatural, work is a curse, and humankind's context is marked by sin, guilt, and punishment. Like Barth, he explicitly rejects that a human capacity such as rationality is associated with the Imago Dei.

Kelsey prefers the Wisdom literature—Proverbs, Ecclesiastes, Song of Solomon, and Job—as the basis for his theological understanding of the relationship between God and people, both because its narrative of creation is pure and not as involved in serving the redemption story and for its focus on the everyday world. "The relation between Creator and creature is best understood as God's being present to creation in hospitable generosity, free delight, and self-determining commitment," he writes.[24]

According to Kelsey, the Wisdom books have an identifiable creation theology. In the Genesis account, Adam and Eve are created already developed. As perfect bodies in Eden, they cannot change. They cannot decline through disease or accident. This presents a problem because it equates being human with perfection. In Wisdom literature, Stephen Plant notes that Kelsey "sees human beings as fragile, vulnerable and finite—and deemed good by God precisely in their fragility, vulnerability, and finitude."[25]

Job was born as an infant, for example, and his maturation involves being formed by the community. His social context teaches him to grow in relation to other humans and God. Further, Job's status is not dependent upon actualizing his capacities and powers, nor imperfections, "nor can it be taken away by any failure to actualize his capacities and exercise his powers appropriately."[26] Job's status is permanent. Kelsey concludes from his reading of Job that there is no absolute standard for human physical, mental, or emotional perfection.[27] These conclusions are relevant to our discussion in chapter 4 about dementia.

Three Anthropological Questions

Kelsey explains that by the mid-twentieth century, three questions arose from the study of our relationship to God.[28] What are we as human creatures? Who am I and who are we (regarding human identity)? How are we to be as faithful creatures (regarding human beings' freedom and responsibility)?

To begin to answer these, Kelsey writes that humans have both a *proximate* and an *ultimate* context. The *proximate* context consists of the finite physical and social worlds in which we live.[29] Our finite nature makes us inherently accident-prone. We inescapably damage each other, we decay, and we undergo hurt, loss, and death. Science as a human endeavor is part of our proximate context. Kelsey notes that for evolution to work, room must be made for successive generations with enhanced fitness; thus death is a part of God's ongoing creativity. What might seem to be undesirable (such as illness or death) is a part of the nature of finite physical reality. Having limits is not an evil, and moral evil is not a consequence of those limits.

On the other hand, there exists an *ultimate* human context, which is the most fundamental and, for Jews, Christians, and Muslims, is "the reality of God and God actively relating."[30]

Question 1: What Are We as Human Creatures?

Kelsey is uncomfortable with the word "person" because it can be used descriptively or normatively. Descriptively, it can be used to classify; for example, this entity is a human person and that one is a dog. In this sense, a being is either a person or not. The word person can also be used normatively, meaning there can be degrees of personhood. So, it is sometimes said, "one may have either more or less fully 'actualized' one's 'real personhood.' "[31] Kelsey rejects this concept because, taken to its limit, there is the possibility of being a "perfect person" with a 100 percent score on all possible degrees of completeness. It is not possible, however, to describe all those degrees making up personhood, nor to establish criteria for the 100 percent score. Because of the complexity of these common usages, Kelsey usually avoids the term "person" altogether.

Next, consider the word "human." The modern secular interpretation of humanity as discussed in chapter 1 would use the criterion of having DNA of the species *Homo sapiens*. Kelsey basically agrees but points out the limits of this definition by applying it to say, a human bone, or human tissue in a Petrie dish—which we would not say is a person—and to the more complicated situation of a fetus.[32] To be clear, he uses the phrase "actual human living bodies" instead of "person." Alternatively, he sometimes uses the adjective "personal," as in "personal living bodies." This definition includes any living human regardless of age, physical or cognitive abilities, sexual organs, or race. His idea is that these attributes in the proximate, everyday world are less important than our ultimate context of relating to God.

God relating to us is what gives us our identity as human creatures, according to Kelsey. It is not physical in nature (we do not lose it with physical injury, for example), nor mental, nor emotional, and we can retain it even when we have deeply compromised ourselves morally. This is reminiscent of Barth's discussion of the human constitution. In all these circumstances, even in the case of severe dementia, for example, God remains in relationship permanently. Kelsey writes:

> By God's gracious creative hospitality, she or he is still, in company with other creatures, God's genuinely "other" partner in a community of discourse, called by God to be wise, and capable of responding in some manner to God, even if only, like many living creatures, by its sheer mute presence before God.[33]

God relates to people through God's creating, drawing us to the end times, and reconciling us through Christ. They have "unqualified dignity and value and deserv[e] unqualified respect solely because they are God's creatures,"[34] Kelsey writes. "Personal bodies are the glory of God."[35]

Kelsey echoes Barth's idea that God is doing most of the work:

> Personhood is not even a function of how we relate to God . . . our personhood is entirely a function of how God relates to us in creating us. . . . The possibility in us of our being addressed by God, our

addressability—and hence, our status as persons—follows excellently from the actuality of God speaking to us, and hardly at all from anything else.[36]

Susannah Cornwall explains, "Kelsey's eccentric locus for human personhood starts from God's relationship to human beings, and is firstly about divine characteristics, not human ones."[37] Kelsey qualifies, however, that "human persons may not act out of that status,"[38] and hence their choices may be disappointing in light of their status.

Kelsey believes that theology must respond to the modern secular interpretation of humanity, which attributes higher human capacities to brain physiology, not to a soul. He invokes neither a rational soul nor the theological concept of the image of God, saying that a soul is not needed for God to relate to human beings. Hebrew Scripture, he notes, lacks the body-soul distinction. God made promises without relating through a human soul. Rather, "God as Creator is no closer to spirit than God is to physical matter."[39]

Significantly, Kelsey believes that the concept of a human is so complex that an exhaustive reduction of it to a set of natural processes is implausible.[40] There is no list of attributes to define what it is to be human. He rejects the argument that humanity differs from animals by self-determination or having language or rationality. These he feels are too narrow, possibly excluding infants and the rationally impaired.

Relationships with other creatures—other humans as well as other living beings—are critical, "so interior to me as to be essential to making me the concretely particular human living body that I am."[41] We help construct others' identities as well. Societal and cultural contexts can sometimes fail to adequately form and nurture some of us. Neediness and desire, however, are a natural part of being a creature and not a failure. We are accountable to show respect for others, which means taking action to nurture their well-being.

Question 2: Who Am I and Who Are We?

For Kelsey, stories describe personal identities, especially stories that tell of actions the person has done that capture his or her essence. They also capture "who . . . persists through change across time."[42] Our stories illustrate the unique ways we love and are loved that make us unsubstitutable.[43]

Kelsey answers the question "Who am I?" by saying "I am 'one radically given to by God.'"[44] A second answer is "I am not isolated," but rather, "I have my personal identity only in giving to others, so that they are to a certain degree inherently dependent on me, and in being given to by others, so that I am inherently dependent on them."[45] Kelsey makes clear that one's personal identity does not depend on others' judgments—rather, it is grounded in God.

Question 3: How Are We to Be as Faithful Creatures?

Wisdom literature calls us to be wise and faithful and to lead healthy, joyful, and prosperous lives. In terms of how we are to be, Kelsey first emphasizes a spirit of gratitude for God's hospitality and loyalty. Second, we are to be aware of our vocation to care for creation. Third, as human living bodies, we are expected to "trust in God as ground of [our] being and value, and as loyalty to God's own creative project."[46] Fourth, we are to love "in both the two distinct enactments of 'love to God' . . . and 'love as neighbour', which is understood as a participation in the triune God's love for us."[47]

God made human beings sufficiently free to fail to live in communion with God, says Kelsey. We are capable of separating ourselves from God, living as if we are in charge. Recognizing the limited time we have, we live on "borrowed breath."[48] In order to flourish, Kelsey believes that human beings are called to take care of themselves, each other, and the earth, knowing that their ultimate context is God's active relationship with us.[49]

Conclusion

In the heart of Kelsey's doctrine, a human being is a "personal living human body" by virtue of God relating to them. God relates to people in three ways: by creating, by redeeming, and by reconciling. Yet Kelsey agrees with science that to be human is to have human DNA and to be a living body, meaning (for him), the umbilical cord is cut. He claims that we are not limited by our physical biological integrity, which can be violated by physical assault and loss of limbs or mobility, nor by our psychological integrity, which can be disrupted for physical, psychodynamic, or chemical reasons, nor by our moral integrity.[50] Dignity and respect follow the simple fact of our being. Even in the case of severe loss, such as coma or severe dementia, people are still capable of responding to God, if only by their "sheer mute living presence before God." Their integrity lies in their "eccentric" nature, with God in the center, rooted in the ways that God relates to them. This is the vertical dimension.

Human creatures are profoundly dependent on other creatures. They actively relate and are actively related to by other creatures in ways that help construct their identities. This is the horizontal dimension. Others' judgments do not define those identities; God's relating defines a human creature's identity.

Kelsey's position is different from historical thinkers that we reviewed, from Plato to Descartes, who often focused on the individual as an ensouled rational animal. Kelsey finds several implications of this view profoundly problematic. He finds that it leads to humans exploiting and devastating other creatures in their own narrow self-interest. It also leads to suspicion, fear, and disparagement of the human body. Kelsey wants to place the flourishing and development of humans in community. Our vocation is to work for its good.

Can personhood be lost? We know that a body can lose awareness or consciousness, a body can change personality (for example, through a brain injury), and a body can lose cognition (as through dementia). Kelsey objects that a human's status is lost because of any physical changes or even because a moral evil has been committed, because a person's relationship with God and with other humans still exists. For Kelsey, the status of personhood is permanent.

Kelsey agrees with science that humans are set apart neither by the Imago Dei nor a soul, but by their distinctive array of capacities including the mental and the emotional, which result from the very complex and hugely connected human brain. But he does not agree with the completely reductionist, secular view of humans; rather he writes of a "complexity in unity" and of God relating to us "creatively to constitute each of us as a unity in complexity."[51]

Reflection Questions

* What is your reaction to David Kelsey's view that God is in the center and always reaching for humans no matter their physical, mental, or moral state?

* How has modern science affected the contemporary theological view of the human person, in particular the concept of the soul? How would you answer the reductionist view that humans are no more than a "bag of neurons"?

* What is your reaction to the argument by some biblical scholars that the term "Image of God" reflects the writer's desire to emphasize that humans were created as royalty (not as a literal image of God)?

* Despite more modern interpretations of a united view of human nature, dualistic ideas about mind and body seem to prevail when the topic of dementia is raised. Why?

* How does the Wisdom literature describe humans, according to Kelsey? How does that affect the way we relate to God?

Notes

1. Stephen G. Post, *The Moral Challenge of Alzheimer Disease* (Baltimore, MD: The Johns Hopkins University Press, 1995), 3.
2. Plato, *The Republic*, trans. B. Jowett (New York: Modern Library, 1941), sect. 435.
3. Ibid., sect. 441.
4. John F. Kutsko, *Between Heaven and Earth: Divine Presence and Absence in the Book of Ezekiel* (Winona Lake, IN: Eisenbrauns, 2000), 60.
5. St. Basil the Great, *On the Human Condition*, trans. Nonna Verna Harrison (Crestwood, NY: St. Vladimir's Seminary Press, 2005), 36.
6. Augustine, *The Confessions*, trans. Maria Boulding, *The Works of Saint Augustine: A Translation for the 21st Century* (Hyde Park NY: New City Press, 1997), 241.
7. Augustine, *The Trinity*, trans. Edmund Hill, *The Works of Saint Augustine: A Translation for the 21st Century*, (Hyde Park, NY: New City Press, 1991), 322.
8. René Descartes, "The Discourse on Method," in *The Philosophical Works of Descartes*, trans. Elizabeth Haldane and G. R. T. Ross (Cambridge: University Press, 1967), 92.
9. Descartes, "Author's Letter," in *The Philosophical Works*, 210.

10. Karl Barth, *Church Dogmatics*, vol. 3, part 2, *Doctrine of Creation 2*, ed. G.W. Bromily and Thomas Torrance (Edinburgh: T&T Clark, 1957-1975), 417.

11. Ibid., part 4, 117.

12. Ibid.., part 1, 195.

13. Karl Barth, *Church Dogmatics*, vol. 2, part 1, *The Doctrine of God*, ed. G.W. Bromily and Thomas Torrance (Edinburgh: T&T Clark, 1957-2004), 273.

14. Barth, vol. 3, part 2, 347.

15. In science/religion debates, it is common to see the term "physicalism," which means that the basis of reality relies on the physical. "Reductive physicalism" means that *everything* reduces to only the physical, an atheistic view. Thus, some would say colloquially that humans are no more than "a bag of neurons." Nancey Murphy distinguishes herself as a "nonreductive physicalist" in that she believes that reality has a physical basis but is in the context of God, culture, and the world.

16. Nancey Murphy, *Bodies and Souls? Or Spirited Bodies?* (New York: Cambridge University Press, 2006), 56.

17. Wesley Wildman, "Spirituality and the Brain: A Scientific Approach to Religious Experience," 2010, accessed March 20, 2017, https://www.youtube.com/watch?v=UHe2oqugSns\.

18. Murphy, 72 (italics added).

19. Ibid., ix (italics added).

20. Ibid., 6.

21. Aubrey Johnson, *The One and the Many in Israelite Conception of God* (Eugene, OR: Wipf and Stock Publishers, 2006), quoted in Murphy, 24.

22. David H. Kelsey, *Eccentric Existence: A Theological Anthropology* (Louisville, KY: Westminster John Knox Press, 2009), 177.

23. Ibid., 181.

24. Ibid., 163.

25. Stephen Plant, "Christian Ethics as Eccentric Existence: On Relating Anthropology and Ethics," *Studies in Christian Ethics* 24, no. 3 (2011): 371.

26. Kelsey, 300.

27. Ibid., 303.

28. David H. Kelsey, "The Human Creature," in *The Oxford Handbook of Systematic Theology*, eds. John Webster and Kathryn Tanner (Oxford: Oxford University Press, 2007), 122.

29. Kelsey, *Eccentric Existence,* 190.

30. Ibid., 5.

31. Ibid., 204.

32. Ibid., 257.

33. Ibid., 282.
34. Ibid., 254.
35. Ibid., 311.
36. Ibid., 296.
37. Susannah Cornwall, "Intersex and the Rhetorics of Disability and Disorder: Multiple and Provisional Significance in Sexed, Gender and Disabled Bodies," *Journal of Disability & Religion* 19 (2015): 110.
38. Kelsey, *Eccentric Existence,* 297.
39. Ibid., 256.
40. Ibid., 284.
41. Ibid., 283.
42. Ibid., 335.
43. Ibid., 391.
44. Ibid., 338.
45. Ibid.
46. Ibid., 310.
47. Tom Greggs, "Article Review: David Kelsey, 'Eccentric Existence: A Theological Anthropology,'" *Scottish Journal of Theology* 65, no. 4 (2012): 455.
48. Kelsey, *Eccentric Existence,* 309.
49. Ibid., 321.
50. Ibid., 282.
51. Ibid., 286.

CHAPTER 4

Theology of Dementia

As discussed in chapter 3, a predominant Western definition of what it is to be a human being was historically associated with the idea of rationality, and this description predisposes society to stigmatize illnesses that cause dementia. More recent theology about being human changes the focus from being an individual with certain attributes to being one in relationship with God. In this chapter, we apply these ideas to dementia.

As noted in the previous chapter, David Kelsey's *Eccentric Existence* is considered a major work in theological anthropology—theological reflections on what it means to be human. Kelsey does not engage in-depth regarding questions of gender, race, sex, class, sexual orientation, and range of abilities or absence of any. He views these attributes as part of everyday personal identities ascribed to people by their cultures and by themselves. He says that whatever hand we are dealt, it is how we live our lives in response to the way God relates to us that is important.

A Theology of Pastoral Care for People with Dementia

In forming a theology of pastoral care for people with dementia, we have chosen to apply six of Kelsey's points from *Eccentric Existence*. First, Kelsey emphasizes that God relates to us, focusing on the person in relationship, not on the person as an individual. Our status as people "follows from the actuality of God speaking to us, and hardly at all from anything else,"[1] even if we are impaired. That relationship is not lost because of dementia or any illness. This is similar to Karl Barth's idea that God's recognition of us depends less on our own particular state, since God is doing most of the work. God continually seeks us more than we seek God. Knowing this is likely to be reassuring to any of us, but especially to those with dementia and their loved ones.

Second, our integrity is preserved even if cognitive abilities fail because God is in relationship with us permanently. Our ability to praise God may be "reduced to sheer mute presence,"[2] but that does not mar the quality of our relationship with God. Kelsey says that people are the glory of God even when their abilities do not develop normally, or when they are lost. Even if words do not come easily, or at all, nothing is lost in the communication as far as God is concerned.[3]

Third, Kelsey moves away from an idealized notion of a "perfect humanity." Humans are by nature finite, and there is nothing evil about having limits. Imperfections do not take away the integrity of who we are. Human dependence and neediness are a part of our nature, and, as Plant put it, we are "deemed good by God precisely in [our] fragility, vulnerability, and finitude."[4] This theological understanding alleviates the stigma of dementia and lightens the burdens of caregivers who often strive imperfectly in their caregiving.

In 1 Corinthians 13:12 Paul writes, "For now we see in a mirror, dimly. . ." We are all blurred and not that different from each other. "The common calling in Christ which disabled and non-disabled share with each other categorically transcends whatever differences they may have from each other," writes theologian Robert Song.[5]

With advances in understanding evolution, we come to see illness and death not as imperfections but as an inherent part of our nature—difficult on an individual level but beneficial for the whole. In this sense, illness and death can be seen as part of God's ongoing creativity.

Fourth, Kelsey unties human uniqueness from a narrow definition of rationality, an idea that has been dominant in Western thought. Kelsey's approach is preferable to equating rationality with the Image of God, which implies that without rationality, the image is damaged or destroyed. Science has shown that making decisions, for example, involves much more than just the rational, thinking parts of the brain.[6] While stating that a list of qualities cannot capture the complexity of a human being, Kelsey appreciates in human neurophysiology: sensation, feeling, emotion, awareness, self-awareness, and consciousness.[7] Emotion, instinct, love, and spirituality—all seen in people with dementia—are human qualities just as important as others.

Fifth, according to Kelsey, we have a vocation to care for the world we live in. We care for others, including those pushed by our society to life's edges, since they contribute to who we are. We are all finite and living on "borrowed breath."[8] Our response to God's creation puts us "more in the position of a steward of a loan than that of an owner of a piece of property."[9] Faith in God "commits us to attitudes, passions, and dispositions that are appropriate responses to that which expresses God's glory."[10] We are accountable to God to respond to the ways God has related to us by how we care for the world and the people in it. Our identities are partly formed by other people, and we help construct their identities as well. Our neediness is not a failure, but part of being a finite creature. The neediness of others allows them to help us be accountable to God. The community is accountable to maintain the identity of those with dementia and enable them to be accountable to God and their neighbors when possible. (Possibilities for service provided by people with dementia are discussed in chapter 7.)

Lastly, Kelsey distinguishes the differences between "flourishing" and having good health: "Flourishing human bodies are not the glory of God because they are healthily flourishing; theologically speaking, they are deemed flourishing to the extent that even in extreme unhealth, they are nonetheless in some mode [derivatively] the glory of God."[11] To flourish is to express God's glory, which gives people a focus that is eccentric—on God, not themselves. We are all asked to live in reverent gratitude, to have faith, to trust in God as the ground of our being, and to love God and neighbor.

Other Voices

In his major work on the theology of dementia, John Swinton "acknowledges the pain and suffering that this condition brings to those with dementia and their families, but offers an alternative theological reading of the condition within which hope and new possibilities—in the present and for the future—remain even in the midst of deep forgetfulness."[12] He writes:

If God is the Creator, and if we live in a creation which God says is good, then at the very least we know that we are created out of love and loved beyond all measure. If God knew us when we were still in the womb (Psalm 139), and if God does have plans for us to prosper, then neurological decline cannot separate us from the love of God and our ongoing vocation as human beings. Lives that are touched by profound forms of dementia have meaning and continuing purpose.[13]

He agrees that personhood is not based on "specific capacities"[14] and that our vocation as humans is to "willfully, intentionally, love one another as God has loved us."[15] He sees dementia as "another example of the limitedness and mortality of the human condition."[16] The illnesses that cause dementia, like other illnesses, "are simply part of what it means to be human beings who are living out their lives in a creation which is broken but in the process of being redeemed."[17] Thus dementia is not a punishment or the work of the devil. It may be difficult to understand why it exists, but it is no different from other illnesses (or injury or aging) in that sense.

A number of theologians have written about disability, and these words fit for people with dementia because it is a kind of disability. "Disabled people still feel tolerated rather than actively welcomed and affirmed," writes Robert Song.[18] He attributes this to their being the objects of other people's projected "buried anxieties about their own vulnerability and encroaching mortality."[19] In the case of dementia, this projection may subconsciously spark fears of aging, dependence, and mortality.

In Christ's suffering we see the "mixed blessing of life and bodies,"[20] and "an acceptance of limits as the truth of being human," writes Nancy Eiesland.[21] We learn from the wounds and disability of Jesus that no illness or aspect that makes us other detracts from our humanity. We do not say that Jesus was less of a human or less of a person on the cross.

Bernd Wannenwetsch takes this further, pointing out that when we recognize one with disability as a person, we in turn discover ourselves as one.

The issue is not one of ascribing rights, as if we were in the quasi-divine position of deciding whether or not to attribute value to someone, but of acknowledging inherent claims on us, taking cognizance of a new fixed point of reference around which we are to organize ourselves. For this reason, people with severe disabilities, rather than being at the margins of the language-game of personhood, are at its centre, for they clarify that human dignity is fundamentally a matter of the humanity that is summoned forth in us as we recognize that we belong together and are called to be with each other.[22]

This argument recalls Kelsey's emphasis that our identities are formed by each other, and that dependence on others is an essential condition of our own integrity. This dependence is mutual for the person with the disability as well as the family member and caregiver. Song writes of the "foundational solidity and non-negotiable presence of disabled people's lives, and therefore *of all human lives.*"[23] Hans Reinders adds that since "the human being exists only as a continued gift of God . . . there is a profound equality of abled and disabled persons in the eyes of God via divine acceptance of their being and a universal drawing-into-communion, so that *acceptance of the other is the only necessary response* when personhood is in question."[24]

Return to the Stories

How does theology change the way we understand the stories we tell of our experiences with people who have dementia? By overvaluing rationality, the two scenarios from the introduction (page xix) describe the detrimental outcomes for the professional (clergy or doctor), the patient, the family, and ultimately society at large. In the first scenario, a clergyperson's visit to a retirement community ended when two of his congregants were "so out of it" that he just said hello and left his card. We assume "out of it" meant the members were cognitively impaired in some way, perhaps temporarily or permanently. Being "out of it" could be interpreted to mean out of the mainstream where everyday norms of rationality dominate. From a theological perspective, "out of it" does not mean out of relationship with God, who is as present as ever, indeed closer to the person than they are to themselves.

Finding his congregation's members in this state was apparently a surprise to the clergyperson. He could have felt upset at seeing the members in this state, accompanied by anxiety rising from his own fears of mortality or dependence. He may have rationalized that the people he was visiting would not know whether or not he tried to communicate beyond a simple hello. From a completely rational view, an attempt to communicate would make no difference. In this view, talking to a person who is "out of it" would be like talking to a stone.

The people he was visiting were very vulnerable. They were alone and might not have known that he was present. He had an opportunity to communicate by praying, reading scripture, or playing music. The attempt could have strengthened his identity and vocation and helped the people he was visiting who needed (perhaps desperately) a connection for maintaining their identity as members of the community. Most important, it is not the people in this situation who are central, but God who is central.

> To care for others and to receive care from others are crucial aspects of human beings' dominion over the earth. That being so, to be in a position where one can only be the recipient of care is not to be in a place that is degrading or indicative of a loss of dignity; it is in fact to be in a holy place, to be part of a fundamental aspect of the human vocation to care for creation. To receive care is a deep reflection of divine love for dependent human beings. To have severe dementia is not in any sense indicative of a loss of dignity or a diminishment of humanness. It is simply a time in a person's life where the human vocation to care for creation takes on a particular form.[25]

Maybe the clergyperson needed training to communicate with a person with special needs. The attempt itself might bring surprising benefits that could actually increase a person's faith. Perhaps he was pressured and in a rush and did not have the patience or emotional strength to make the effort. Clergy also cannot be expected to meet every challenge, because they are fragile, finite, and vulnerable themselves.

In the second scenario, a doctor's behavior toward Jane, a person who has severe dementia, and her family reflected a dehumanizing ethic. Jane was treated disrespectfully, as if she were invisible. The doctor made "logical" assumptions that she could not understand his words or interpret his tone of voice. This led to an insensitive conversation about hospice decisions as if she were not there. His question, "What are you keeping her alive for?" revealed his inability to see past Jane's dementia to a person beloved by God. Before the family could object, he mocked her by shouting in her face, "What do you do for fun, Jane?" Knowing that she could not answer, he implied that she had little if any quality of life. In fact, she grimaced, registering displeasure.

It could be that the doctor was projecting his own anxiety about loss of control. His approach implied that if he cannot have life on his own terms, it is not worth living. But Jane was not alone; her family was there. The doctor had an opportunity to be empathetic to her and her family, all of whom felt stressed about the hospital visit. He could also have provided helpful advice to the family (in private) based on medical knowledge. The interaction could have strengthened his identity and vocation. It also could have benefitted Jane and her family members, who had been struggling with the illness for many years.

Conclusion

People with dementia are still people, beloved by God. Our narrative and our relationships are broad enough to maintain that identity. God continues actively to relate to all of us, despite our frailties. Dementia is a brain disease, nothing more and nothing less. The brain in those with dementia is still operating in a fierce way. Billions of pieces of information—among them vision, hearing, smells, touch, and taste—are still being transmitted, even if impaired.

The community holds the everyday identity of those within it, including those with dementia or any other disability. Accepting a person with a disability provides what Song calls the "foundational solidity and non-negotiable presence of disabled people's lives, and therefore *of all human lives.*"[26] That acceptance is how we respond in faith, hope, and love, while still honoring the sense of loss and grief of those with dementia and their families. It is a pain worthy of our grief.

Reflection Questions

* Whether a person identifies as a person of faith, an atheist, or in between, does dementia have an impact on this aspect of her or his identity?

* How can we use these insights for better care and better advocacy for people with dementia, and for improving end-of-life decisions?

* How does Kelsey's focus on relationship with God affect a person's integrity? Does this give you hope? Why?

* How can your faith community maintain the identity of those with dementia who are in its midst?

* What more do these insights teach us about our own sense of self in relation to God?

Notes

1. David H. Kelsey, *Eccentric Existence: A Theological Anthropology* (Louisville, KY: Westminster John Knox Press, 2009), 296.
2. Ibid., 282.
3. Ibid., 345.
4. Stephen Plant, "Christian Ethics as Eccentric Existence: On Relating Anthropology and Ethics," *Studies in Christian Ethics* 14, no. 3 (2011): 371.
5. Robert Song, "Conclusion: Fragility and Grace; Theology and Disability," in *Theology, Disability and the New Genetics: Why Science Needs the Church*, eds. John Swinton and Brian Brock (London: T&T Clark, 2007), 243.
6. Joshua Greene et al., "An fMRI Investigation of Emotional Engagement in Moral Judgment," *Science* 293 (2001): 2105-2108.
7. Kelsey, *Eccentric Existence*, 540.
8. Ibid., 309.
9. Ibid., 209.
10. Ibid., 311.
11. Ibid., 317.
12. John Swinton, *Dementia: Living in the Memories of God* (Grand Rapids, MI: William Eerdmans Publishing Company, 2012), 17.
13. Ibid., 20.
14. Ibid., 160.
15. Ibid., 181.
16. Ibid., 186.
17. Ibid., 183.
18. Song, 239.
19. Ibid., 240.
20. Nancy Eiesland, *The Disabled God: Toward a Liberatory Theology of Disability* (Nashville: Abingdon Press, 1994), 102.
21. Ibid., 103.
22. Bernd Wannenwetcsh, quoted in Song, 241.
23. Song, 242 (italics added).
24. Hans Reinders, cited by Susannah Cornwall, "Intersex and the Rhetorics of Disability and Disorder: Multiple and Provisional Significance in Sexed, Gender and Disabled Bodies," *Journal of Disablity and Religion* 19 (2015): 116 (italics added).
25. Swinton, 171.
26. Song, 242 (italics added).

CHAPTER 5

Aging and Spirituality

Each stage and phase of life is ordained by God and therefore has a purpose. We grow in never-ending spirals of change, as the progression of our lives ebbs and flows, with the Spirit nudging and guiding us always. There is no one phase of life that is more important than another: each has its place; each is equally essential . . . ongoing faith formation throughout life supports a spirituality that is constantly growing, ever changing.[1]

If no one phase of life is more important than another, why does American culture resist so strongly the idea of growing old? The messages from the media, families, and even churches are overwhelming: aging is to be avoided at all costs. Physically, older people can alter the effects of aging on their bodies through surgery, Botox, creams, and lotions. They can push retirement back and keep working well into their seventies or even into their eighties.

They can eat healthy diets, exercise regularly, and keep the pace of life unaltered. None of these are bad things to do; they are unarguably important for the future. But are people missing anything in life by continually avoiding the next phase that "has its place [and] is equally essential"?

Who are these people who make up the next phase of life? Like the population in general, they represent all races, cultures, and beliefs. Those identities color how they move through the landscape of aging and how families and friends treat them. Irrespective of their backgrounds, we still want to avoid what author Susan Jacoby describes as the "disingenuous practice of lumping together all people over sixty-five."[2]

Lumping together sixty-five-, seventy-five-, and eighty-five-year-olds to describe their physiological and psychological condition makes as much sense as lumping together five-, fifteen-, and twenty-year-olds. When we describe the health of "people over sixty-five," we blithely note that only 5 percent are confined to nursing homes. But when we focus on the eighty-five-plus age group, the likelihood of spending time in a nursing home jumps to 50 percent.

The "Young Old" (ages sixty-five to seventy-four) includes the first wave of aging Baby Boomers who reached full retirement age in January 2011. Because of health and other considerations, many now consider this middle age. For many, it is a time of good health and the freedom to explore new paths. Milton Crum, who chronicled his aging in two monographs (*I'm Old* and *I'm Frail)*, described this time with his wife as the best days of their lives. As another writer noted, "We can still do *anything* we truly desire to do even though we can no longer do *everything* we want."[3]

The "Older Old" (ages seventy-four to eighty-four) is relatively small compared to the rising boomers, although people in this category rarely see themselves as "old." By 2021 boomers will be entering this age group. They are predicted to change expectations that culture and society have for this cohort as they move up. This is a middle stage, still defined by the first stage, health, and how certain tasks are accomplished. It moves individuals into the final stage, sometimes slowly and gently, and at other times swiftly and relentlessly.

The "Oldest-Old" (eighty-five+) is the fastest-growing segment of the total population in the United States. Now 10 percent of the older population, this cohort is expected to more than triple from 5.7 million in 2010 to over 19 million by 2050.[4] Some call it the "winter" of life, a time when many must relinquish much that they have considered essential. Bodies may no longer do their bidding, and they may be dependent on others for life itself.

People over eighty-five say that aging is a gradual process that often creeps up with little fanfare.

In her book *The Third Chapter*, educational sociologist Sara Lawrence-Lightfoot says, "The developmental terrain grows more layered; patience trumps speed; restraint trumps ambition; wisdom trumps IQ; 'leaving a legacy' trumps 'making our mark'; and a bit of humor saves us all."[5]

✳ ✳ ✳

In his obituary, the professional accomplishments of a man were dutifully listed. In addition to a distinguished military career, he had worked as a lawyer for several government agencies, winning several recognitions and awards for his service. He had made his mark in many significant ways.

After retirement, however, he began building his legacy. He became a volunteer at a nearby middle school, teaching young boys the art of chess. He used his skills as a lawyer to represent families and children in court and to serve as their advocate and advisor. Several weekends each summer, he would load his grandkids in the car for trips to the beach. No other adults were allowed to accompany them. The obituary also included the names of his survivors. I wonder what was more important to them: his "mark" or his "legacy"?—Dorothy

✳ ✳ ✳

Never before in human history has our planet contained so many older people, or such a large percentage of them. Increased life expectancies and energetic lifestyles now enable many to live 20 to 25 percent of their lives in active retirement. By the time the last boomers turn sixty-five in 2029, one in five Americans will be sixty-five or older.[6] By 2042 the population will be majority minority—more than half the population will be non-white or Latino. Racial and ethnic groups continue to differ on important age-related metrics, including life expectancy, living arrangements, disease prevalence, income levels, and poverty rates. As noted in chapter 2, a higher incidence of Alzheimer's disease among older African Americans, for example, is a reality.

Physical Changes

The spiritual life is not disconnected from the changes that aging brings to bodies, including health and emotional stability. During young adulthood, most physiological and physical functions are at their most efficient levels. By the middle to late twenties, the majority of physical growth and development of muscles, internal organs, and body systems have reached a plateau for most people. During their forties and fifties, people start noticing physical changes that affect both behavior and performance. By the time people reach their sixties, almost all individuals have one or more chronic conditions to contend with.

Often the external and observable changes, such as gray hair and wrinkles caused by a decrease in the flexibility of collagen fibers, remind people that they are aging. The muscular system begins to change noticeably as people reach their mid-thirties, including changes in overall muscle strength, muscle mass and tone, and the redistribution of fat. As people age, flexibility in connective tissues and joints decreases, while bones weaken and are more easily broken. At about age twenty-five, the heart rate is at its peak efficiency, losing about 1 percent of its reserve pumping capacity each year after age thirty, thus reducing the amount of oxygen delivered to tissues. Many of the debilitating effects of cardiovascular changes are the result of disease, however, and not a consequence of normal aging.[7]

The maximum breathing or vital capacity of the lungs decreases progressively between twenty and sixty years of age, due to a loss of elasticity in the joints of the rib cage and the lung tissue itself, along with weakened muscles that support the lungs. The digestive system works less efficiently due to slower action of the muscles, reduced acid production, and impaired ability to absorb nutrients. Metabolism begins to slow around age twenty-five, and most people gain weight even when being careful about diet and exercise.[8]

The ability to think, reason, and act in response to incoming stimulation from the environment depends on the integrity of the central nervous system, which is composed of the brain and the spinal cord. As discussed in chapter 1, research about this system keeps adding to our understanding of how the brain works and how we access memories. This work may lead to a cure for Alzheimer's and other related diseases, in addition to slowing down the damage disease causes in the brain.

A deceptive myth about aging leads people to believe that as long as they eat right, exercise, and stay healthy, they will dance their way into and through old age. Boomers in particular, some of whom are now in their seventies, embrace this line of reasoning. Writers like Milton Crum debunk this rosy picture: "My illusion was that, if I took proper care of my body, as the years passed, I would become the still-vigorous *wellderly*, not the *illderly*."[9] In *I'm Frail,* written three years later, he defines frailty as a "condition, sometimes lasting years, that most old people endure before death during which various ailments conspire to make death more attractive than life."[10] His summation of the last years of his life hardly seems "graceful."

Many boomers, especially those born before the late 1950s, not only believe that they will be among Milton Crum's "wellderly," but also avoid all references to retirement or slowing down. If they don't talk about bodies getting older, they can ignore the new aches and pains that creep up on them. At a church gathering, several older boomers noted with a chuckle that the first thing most recent retirees accomplish is surgery on knees, hips, or other joints. The wear and tear on bodies forces older people to slow down and set their sights a little lower.

Depression and Substance Abuse

The American culture's negative view of aging sometimes skews perceptions about the prevalence of depression among older people. The good news is that the majority of older adults are *not* depressed. Some estimates of major depression in older people range from less than 1 percent to about 5 percent, but rise significantly among those who require home healthcare or hospitalization.[11] At the same time about 80 percent of adults over sixty-five have at least one chronic health condition, and 50 percent have two or more. Depression is more likely to occur in people who also have other illnesses (such as heart disease or cancer) or whose function becomes limited.[12]

Too often healthcare providers mistake an older adult's symptoms of depression as a natural reaction to illness or the life changes that occur with aging, and therefore do not see depression as something to be treated. Older adults, especially those over seventy-five, often share this belief and do not seek help because they don't realize that they could feel better. Depression is a true and treatable medical condition that is not a normal part of aging, although older adults are at an increased risk for experiencing it. Depression is not just having "the blues" or the emotions felt when grieving the loss of a loved one. It is a medical condition that is treatable, like diabetes or hypertension.

Some aspects of mental health improve with age. Adults who are sixty-five or older are less likely to have a form of mental illness than other age groups from eighteen to sixty-four. Suicide rates for older people are less than half the national average. However, many older adults still experience mental distress associated with limitations in daily activities, physical impairments, grief following loss of loved ones, caregiving or challenging living situations, or an untreated mental illness such as depression.[13]

Population research shows that there are more than 2.5 million adults over sixty-five with an alcohol or drug problem. Older adults are hospitalized as often for alcohol-related problems as for heart attacks. Although people sixty-five years of age and older make up only 13 percent of the population, they account for almost 30 percent of all medications prescribed in the United States.[14] As a result, older adults are at risk for prescription drug abuse and addiction. In addition to prescription medications, many older adults also use over-the-counter medicines, vitamins, and dietary supplements, which cause problems as the body is less able to process medications and the potential of negative drug interactions increases.

The national crisis in the overuse of opioids has also had an impact on older populations. In the late 1990s the medical community began to monitor pain as a fifth vital sign in addition to temperature, heartbeat, breathing rate, and blood pressure. Some attribute the dramatic rise in the use of prescription painkillers among all age groups, including those over sixty-five, to the change in patient monitoring. Older people have been conditioned to turn to drugs for relief, whether an over-the-counter drug to calm an inflamed joint or an opioid to ease major pain. Americans in 2016 filled over four billion prescriptions at retail pharmacies; adults over sixty-five filled more than twice as many prescriptions as those under sixty-five.[15] Regardless of intentions, lack of communication among care providers, or mental health issues, the destructive results of addiction are the same for all ages.[16]

Because of insufficient knowledge, limited research data, and hurried office visits, alcohol and drug misuse and abuse among older adults are often overlooked. Diagnoses may be difficult because symptoms of alcoholism and drug dependency in older people sometimes mimic those of other medical and behavioral disorders common among this population, such as diabetes, dementia, and depression. There is an unspoken but pervasive assumption that it's not worth treating older adults for substance use disorders. "What difference does it make; they won't be around much longer anyway." Behavior considered a problem in younger people does not inspire the same urgency for older adults. Along with the impression that alcohol or substance abuse problems cannot be successfully treated in older adults, especially those diagnosed with some form of dementia, there is also the assumption that treatment for this population is a waste of healthcare resources.

Satisfaction Amid Change and Loss

Elaine Brody, a well-known gerontologist, reflected on her work and her own experience of aging toward the end of her life in an article for *The Gerontologist.* Born in 1922, she lived through the Great Depression and socioeconomic developments, such as Social Security, Medicare, Medicaid, and Supplemental Security Income. All had a profound impact on the field of aging. Reflecting on the changes in the terrain of working with the elderly, Brody noted that she passed through the stages of young-old, then old-old, to reach very old.

> We are different from the very old of the past. We have had more educa-
> tion and better health care since early childhood. Many more women
> in our age group have done out-of-home work than did our mothers.
> Transportation, communication, and technology have exploded in our
> lifetimes (although some of us do have trouble with the latter). We, the
> very very old, are a new frontier—for ourselves and for you to know and
> understand.[17]

The one habit she never broke was that of listening. Although she was no longer a social worker or researcher later in life, she remained eager to hear the stories of her friends and peers, including their concerns and worries, problems and joys. Brody noted that she doesn't remember becoming old. Her waistline thickened, her hair thinned, and balance "was not great." She added:

> My present perspective, then, is that of an 86-year-old woman who, I
> suppose, was prepared for old age intellectually but not emotionally.

Even my children are growing into the stages of life I studied. Common experiences of old age, such as illness and losses, were unexpected, even though expectable.[18]

The most significant aspect of emotional change may be dealing with loss, which Brody found to be pervasive as a person grows older. Loss comes with the death of a spouse or close friend, the loss of identity for people for whom work defined their lives, changes in lifestyles, and moving into new residences. As older people approach their own deaths, questions pushed down about bigger issues begin to rise of their own accord as these individuals deal with the unexpectedness of the expectable.

Focusing on loss can mask the contentment many older people describe. New studies are overturning stereotypes about our culture and how "gifts, charms, and joys flow mostly to the young."[19] Studies that actually measure happiness show that the elderly often come out ahead. We see the losses older people endure in health, self-sufficiency, friends, and loved ones and assume they are depressed and unhappy. But they also report less anxiety and difficulties with finances, interpersonal relationships, and crime. "Our research reveals that well-being gets better with age. People seventy-five and older have even higher well-being than those sixty-five to seventy-four, and they outscore their younger counterparts by a sizable margin."[20]

People who work past sixty-five also are, for the most part, more satisfied with their jobs than younger workers. That older people may be happier seems to be counter to studies that show them at a higher risk for depression and other mental health problems.

> Older Americans also have higher well-being across each of the five elements of well-being: purpose, social, financial, community, and physical. Older Americans score especially high in financial well-being . . . and express more satisfaction with their standard of living, worry less about money, and say they have enough money to do what they want to do—all at higher rates than their younger counterparts. Older Americans also have better access to healthcare than those under the age of fifty-five, with higher rates of having health insurance, a personal doctor, and access to medicine than younger people.[21]

The General Social Survey, which has been monitoring societal change and studying American society since 1972, has data that consistently shows older people are happier than younger adults.[22] Researchers looked at the data more closely in 2008 to discover why. The results ran counter to expectations that illnesses, deaths, and other losses of older people would result in a greater unhappiness in life. Older survey respondents reported far fewer difficulties overall financially and personally. Younger adults meanwhile had less trouble with their health, but more of other kinds of predicaments.

Other researchers using these data found that advanced age was correlated with feeling positive. It is not that older adults do not have negative emotions, they discovered, but when they are negative, they are passive. While older people reported more loneliness, they also indicated much more serenity. Higher levels of depression in older people, researchers concluded, don't come from negative emotions, but from higher levels of passivity.[23]

Spirituality of Our Selves

The spirituality of a person is not an isolated dimension in life because it permeates and gives meaning to all life. It is the deepest dimension of all of humanity's existence through all of its intricacies.[24] The opposite of spiritual well-being is fragmentation and isolation. When asked to define spirituality, people often respond—following an embarrassed silence—with phrases that might include the words "nature," "a specific experience," and maybe even "God" and "relationship." Although spirituality is often listed in surveys and profiles as "very important," few are able to describe it.

Robert Atchley suggests that spirituality takes three basic forms: "intense awareness of the present, transcendence of the personal self, or a feeling of connection with all of life, the universe, a supreme being, or a great web of being."[25] These basic forms are based on a series of questions, such as "What does it mean to grow spiritually?" or "What is the nature of a spiritual journey?" or "How does spirituality manifest itself in everyday life?" These kinds of questions come from people trying to move into a deeper relationship with God.

✳ ✳ ✳

Sometimes as people reach very old age they begin to wonder why they are still around. A deeply beloved matriarch of a family began asking that question. She had entered ordained ministry in her sixties and served in that capacity for almost thirty years. Her family, which included her children, grandchildren, great-grandchildren, and all of their significant others, still loved being with her, basking in her wisdom and reveling in the gracefulness in which she lived her life. But recently she began apologizing for her inability to get around on her own and raised the question on more than one occasion about what purpose she served.

The Missionaries of Charity, the order of nuns founded by Mother Teresa, believe the greatest gift we can offer to each other is our vulnerability. By allowing others to care for our needs, we give them the chance to see Christ and to be Christ. The answer to the difficult question about the usefulness of life when a person is frail and perhaps even living with dementia runs counter to our culture's values, which is why it is so difficult to comprehend. But maybe these faithful nuns who take on the care of the outcast and needy are right: our vulnerability is our gift to those we love.—*Dorothy*

✳ ✳ ✳

People who have been on spiritual journeys for years "usually have developed a sense of humor about the contradictions and paradoxes they encounter," says Atchley.[26] They also discover that they can't force the issue. "Waiting is an important spiritual practice," he adds, "not 'waiting for' but just waiting. In the space created by patient waiting, connection with the sacred or 'ground of being' is more likely." Just as the family matriarch questioned her purpose in life, many older people believe they have lived beyond their perceived "usefulness."

Atchley's three forms of spirituality, which are relevant to all people of all ages, are guideposts for how faith communities can create programs, events, liturgies, and prayers in order to move into a deeper relationship with God. A greater understanding of spirituality will not only help congregations serve their aging members, but also provide more meaningful relationships among children, youth, and adults.

A person is much more than the sum of their intellect, social being, and physical body. "Intertwined and energizing all of [their] integral parts is their kinship with God."[27] How do people know if they have spiritual well-being? It is more than physical, psychological, or social good health. It is an affirmation of life: the ability to say "yes" to life in spite of negative circumstances. This is not a Pollyanna form of optimism that denies the realities of loss; rather, it is the acknowledgment of destiny in life.

That destiny includes the love of a person's own life and the lives of others, along with concern for the community, society, and all of creation. The affirmation of life that comes from the dynamic of spiritual well-being is grounded in life in community. Within that community, people grow to accept the past, live into the present, and seek the hope of life in the future.

"Spirituality, or lack of it, is present in all of the challenges of the older man or woman of God—from changing of multiple roles, declining health, losses of life-long partners, seeking to ascertain self-worth, making new friends, to anticipation of the end of our earthly existence."[28] Christians believe that life has significance through relationship with God. It is within this relationship that we find meaning in life, spiritual fulfillment, and unity.

Finding Our Selves

Franciscan brother Richard Rohr, in *Falling Upward: A Spirituality for the Two Halves of Life,* says:

> There are two major tasks to human life. The task of the first half of life is to create a proper container for one's life and answer some central questions. 'Who am I?' 'What makes me significant?' 'How can I support myself?' 'Who will go with me?' The task of the second half of life is, quite simply, to find the actual contents that this container was meant to hold and deliver. In other words, the container is for the sake of the contents.[29]

For many, though not all, the task of filling the container begins during the latter part of life, as they begin to slow down and look for deeper meaning in life. Bodies are changing, containers are either made or under construction, and spiritual needs are shifting. Where do people find a deeper sense of how those seemingly disparate parts of life come together in unity?

Life Review

In 1963, Robert Butler strongly defended as healthy the tendency of older people to slip into old memories, and he gave it a name: life review. He argued that this tendency was a "naturally occurring, universal mental process characterized by the progressive return to consciousness of past experience, and particularly, the resurgence of unresolved conflicts; simultaneously, and normally, these revived experiences and conflicts can be surveyed and reintegrated . . . prompted by the realization of approaching dissolution and death, and the inability to maintain one's sense of personal invulnerability."[30]

James Thorson takes Butler's ideas about life review a step further and more personally. The life review, writes Thorson, "is in a sense a process of rationalization in which we can persuade ourselves that we've led pretty good lives." He tells his students that when they listen to older people, they aren't required to correct historical misinterpretations and that they have the power to give absolution. "This latter point astonishes them. I assure them that people who are hung up on a problem or guilty about past actions just might benefit from absolution, from a listener telling them, 'I don't think you're such a stinker.' "[31]

Hidden Learning

As people grow older, old habits and self-perceptions still color how they see themselves and relate to others. This fact is not altered initially by the intrusion of dementia into a person's life. Dysfunctional families do not change their behaviors quickly, if at all, and broken relationships do not miraculously mend. Opposite views about decisions that must be made by families can increase division even more.

A factor that keeps people from knowing themselves and understanding their complex relationships with others is "hidden learning." Psychologist Bruce Stevens writes, "Hidden learning is anything we have learned through experience but lack words to express. . . . So what we first learn is initially inarticulate or 'hidden.' It may be right or wrong or a bit of both. But because it is *learned*, it will always feel *true*."[32] He argues that hidden learning begins in early childhood at about eighteen months of age, before a person even begins to speak. The earliest assumptions about people and the way life works may already be set in place by then, before they had any capacity for language. Hidden learning, he says, may lack words, but will always feel true. Understandings about life are already "laid down like railway tracks before words formed in their mind. Hidden learning is simply a way of learning about what is 'normal' in life, how to act and how to treat others. It is not about truth because this knowing is often dysfunctional."[33]

People continue to increase their hidden learning throughout life, says Stevens, although it is learning that is often assumed, rather than contemplated. Stevens calls this "lazy learning" because it depends on unconscious assumptions rather than thinking about life in a coherent way. Since words are not attached to hidden learning, it becomes more powerful and determines how people act as adults. "When we assume a truth," says Stevens, "it becomes 'sacred.' We cannot dispute it. This will bypass the way we think about our beliefs . . . so hidden learning determines behavior unconsciously."[34] It becomes an "expressed truth" about a person that defines his or her identity.

* * *

My dad was the youngest of three sons, and he had polio as an infant, which caused his muscles to atrophy on one side of his chest. That he survived was a miracle. His older brothers always treated him with slight disdain, which I picked up on even as a child. Dad's mother died when he was very young, and all four males in the family were highly competitive and aggressive. Before he could even speak, hidden learning began to determine his behavior. He had to try harder mentally and physically to prove himself worthy in this family.

My dad definitely had a type A personality by the time he was an adult. He was very organized, ambitious, impatient, and highly aware of time management. He was never late for anything, even after retirement, and kept meticulous records. His lifestyle also resulted in stress-related symptoms such as insomnia and indigestion, adding to the tension in our family.

During the early stages of dementia, he responded to memory loss with careful note-taking, such as taping lengthy notes to the washing machine about how to do a load of laundry. Then one day I got a call from his best friend about dad not being ready for a planned outing. It wasn't that he was late that worried his friend; it was his lack of concern about his lateness. He just didn't seem to care.

A lifetime of hidden learning didn't immediately fade away, but we watched him slowly set aside his need to be aggressive and impatient. Dementia uncovered for us a gentler soul that had probably always been present, but rarely seen.—*Dorothy*

* * *

After first applying the concept of hidden learning to intimate relation-ships, Stevens later expanded it to spiritual care of older people through a life tasks model. A life task, says Stevens, is a responsibility that lasts a lifetime after it has begun.[35] The first task is discovering the hidden learning, and the second is to test that discovery with life experiences. The final task is an inte-gration of experiences that leads to greater awareness and a more cohesive self. This self-awareness will ideally lead to service or vocation.[36] A person with dementia is unlikely to complete these tasks, but may still move along the life task spectrum as hidden learning is forgotten and a different persona based on life experience emerges.

Erikson's Stages of Development

Erik Erikson, a developmental theorist who spent a long time coming to terms with his identity, was surprised by life when he got older. The descrip-tions he had so carefully given to Stage 8, the elder years, didn't match his own experiences as he became very old. From his earlier descriptions of life stages, the eighth stage was to be the final crisis, but there was a quality of life, or lack of quality, that he had not foreseen.

By the time people are in their seventies, they are fully engaged in Erikson's eighth stage, pitting integrity against despair. The definition he uses for integ-rity is not an esoteric description of moral principle; it is much deeper and robust. Integrity results in bringing together all the preceding stages of life, adapting to the "triumphs and disappointments," and gradually growing the fruit of oneness.[37] Another important dimension to Erikson's eighth stage is wisdom, defined by Joan Erikson, his wife and collaborator, as the "capacity to see, look, and remember, as well as to listen, hear, and remember." Integrity and wisdom, the positive outcome of Stage 8, "demands tact, contact, and touch."[38] In the final chapter in the extended version of *The Life Cycle Completed,* Joan Erikson writes,

> Life in the eighth stage includes a retrospective accounting of one's life to date; how much one embraces life as having been well-lived, as opposed to regretting missed opportunities, will contribute to the degree of dis-gust and despair one experiences. As Erik has reminded us, "Despair

expresses the feeling that the time is now short, too short for the attempt to start another life and try out alternate roads."[39]

As Erikson lived into the ninth decade himself, he and Joan identified a ninth stage not long before he died at age ninety-one. Stage 9 explores the reality of aging beyond the community life that is so much a part of the other eight stages. Folding in Buddhist ideas with Western psychology, Joan Erikson goes further to describe a transcendence that encompasses the losses of old age and the search for meaning. She argues that by the ninth and tenth decades of life, many people do not have the luxury or desire for the internal despair they wrestled with in Stage 8.[40]

As people approach their nineties, they "have one firm foothold to depend on." Joan Erikson believes that people are blessed with basic trust from the beginning of life if they successfully navigate the first of Erikson's stages that begins in infancy with the crisis of trust vs. mistrust. Without trust, she says, "life is impossible, and with it we have endured . . . it has accompanied and bolstered us with hope . . . no matter how severely hope has been challenged, it has never abandoned us completely."[41]

Hope and Wisdom

In a list of "12 requests from someone with Alzheimer's," the Center for Aging Alzheimer's Family Support Program at Duke University Medical Center includes "Remember my future. I need hope for tomorrow."[42] Hope can be nurtured by building on trust experienced throughout life for people of any age, suffering brain disease or not.

Donald Capps, a developmental theorist, says that the "wise self" of older people comes from their ability to jettison some of the rules and regulations that have bound their lives. He suggests that gracefulness becomes a new dynamic for people in their eighties and nineties, "a worthy successor to wisdom"[43] that had once been so revered. "In art, for example, painters in their later years do not necessarily change their styles as much as they embrace the freedom to move into new space. Wisdom does not necessarily come from more years of experience than those who are younger but from a perspective that is liberated from the rules, roles, and rituals of the past."[44]

✳ ✳ ✳

My dad, whom I always felt was wise, moved into a "gracefulness" that puzzled and alarmed me at first, but eventually became his new expression of wisdom. All his life, he had been bound by time and responsibility to family, work, church, and friends.

As Alzheimer's disease began to play out, he became more mellow. Being late stopped being a cardinal sin. The complexities of a washing machine stopped being an issue when he stopped washing his clothes. A shrug of his shoulders accompanied by a slow grin replaced the intensity of his old demeanor and defined his new self.

Dad's expectations for others also softened. The grace he extended to himself was also offered to others.—*Dorothy*

* * *

From a very practical standpoint, Capps says that wisdom is "not equated with esoteric knowledge or abstract theories. Rather it is practical, sensible, and capable of explaining why wisdom provides a person the authority to recommend *this* over *that* course of action."[45] People come to accept courses of action no longer within their control.

Disengagement vs. Activity

At about the same time the Eriksons were probing their new ninth stage of development, other theorists, such as Lars Tornstam in Sweden, were making similar observations. The word that arose from their findings is gerotranscendence, a disengagement theory that arose in the 1980s to describe how people maintain hope when coping with frailty and other challenges. Gerotranscendence comes from the words "gero" ("old age," in Greek) and "transcendence" ("to climb over," in Latin). Tornstam saw it as a shift "from a materialistic and rational vision to a more cosmic and transcendent one, normally followed by an increase in life satisfaction."[46] The Eriksons describe an almost complete regression at the end of life,[47] while Tornstam describes it as an ascension.[48] Ironically, their conclusions come from very similar observations.

Tornstam uses Erikson's stage development theory as a starting point and considers gerotranscendence—if achieved—to be the final stage of developing toward wisdom.[49] In an interview with the *New York Times*, Tornstam told a story to illustrate the term. He began by describing a hypothetical daughter planning a cocktail party. Her elderly mother usually attended these gatherings and enjoyed herself, so the daughter invited her as usual. This time, however, the mother declined. Not surprisingly, the daughter worried, wondering if her mother was ill or depressed. She had always jumped at this kind of invitation in the past. But perhaps there's nothing wrong, said Dr. Tornstam, who has been investigating aging for more than twenty-five years. Our values and interests don't usually remain static from the time we're twenty years old until the time we're forty-five, so why do we expect that sort of consistency in later decades? "We develop and change; we mature," he told me in a phone interview from his home in Uppsala, Sweden. "It's a process that goes on all our lives, and it doesn't ever end. The mistake we make in middle age is thinking that good aging means continuing to be the way we were at fifty. Maybe it's not."[50]

Tornstam argues that an older person's increased need for solitude and the company of a few close friends is a trait of a continuing maturation. From his perspective the daughter's mother isn't necessarily deteriorating, she's evolving. "People tell us they are different people at eighty," Tornstam explained. "They have new interests, and they have left some things behind."[51]

Gerotranscendent elders are less self-occupied and more altruistic. As they age, they often become more selective in their choices of social and other activities, avoiding social interactions they judge to be unnecessary. Gerotranscendent seniors report a decreased interest in material things, viewing too many possessions as burdensome.

They express a greater need for "alone time" for thought and meditation, referred to as "positive solitude." Gerotranscendent elders remove their "masks" because they no longer feel the need to play their old roles; they can now be themselves. These individuals find themselves simply accepting the mysteries of life, acknowledging they can't understand everything. When gerotranscendent older adults reflect on their lives, they realize that their pieces of life's jigsaw puzzle really do form a wholeness.

Gerotranscendence brings with it changing perceptions of time. An elder may report that he or she experiences feelings of being a child, a young person, an adult, and an older adult all in one moment.

✳ ✳ ✳

One afternoon in late spring I sat near an open window at my kitchen table and felt a very muggy breeze stroke my face. In the distance, I could hear the sounds of children at play. It was a drowsy, comfortable place to be, so I shut my eyes. All of a sudden I could smell food cooking and hear the rattle of pans, the opening and shutting of drawers, and footsteps.

For a brief moment I was a child again, feeling at ease in the security of my room at my childhood home in Oklahoma. I was transported back in time by memories of the familiar sounds and aromas of my mother fixing dinner. The sounds of the children playing nearby invaded my senses briefly before I willfully turned back to that other place where I was a child again.

When I had this experience, my mother was no longer alive, and the home of my childhood was just a distant memory. Our minds, we are told by Lars Tornstam and others, are capable of transcending time and space to follow our memories and maybe even our longings. When I returned to the present, I discovered with the psalmist that my soul was calmed and quieted, "like a child quieted at its mother's breast." Psalm 131:2 (RSV)—*Dorothy*

* * *

Finally, gerotranscendent individuals view death as a natural part of the life process, often fearing death less than those who are younger.

To summarize Tornstam's ideas about the way gerotranscendence affects individuals:

- There is an increased feeling of affinity with past generations and a decreased interest in superfluous social interaction.
- There is often a feeling of cosmic awareness, and a redefinition of time, space, life, and death.
- The individual becomes less self-occupied and at the same time more selective in the choice of social and other activities. Solitude becomes more attractive.
- The individual might also experience a decrease in interest in material things.

A continued debate about the best ways for older people to face the challenges of aging pits disengagement theorists like Tornstam against "activity theory." Disengagement encourages withdrawal from social activities to help "the individual prepare for death by loosening their emotional bounds with others."[52] Activity theory espouses the exact opposite.

* * *

Bob is a ninety-five-year-old friend who still lives alone on a farm in Oklahoma, rides horses, and goes on trail rides. He firmly believes in activity theory. Until recently, he remained active in his profession as a PhD chemist, traveling as a consultant throughout the country. He argues that an active life with intellectual pursuits and physical exercise will stave off dementia and poor health. Although his wife died of Alzheimer's disease over ten years ago, he believes an active life could forestall even that disease.—*Dorothy*

* * *

While disengagement may seem attractive to those leading busy lives with too many checklists and demanding schedules, pulling away from social contact can lead to depression and substance abuse, as noted earlier. There are compelling reasons for staying connected to communities, which provide support, and for the work of activity directors at retirement communities.

Happiness Among Older Adults

Despite growing concern about the incidence of depression and alcohol and drug abuse among older people, they are less likely to be *victims* of the realities of life, argues Froma Walsh, and more likely to be resilient, with the ability to shape as well as to be shaped by events.[53] She believes their ability to transcend current realities provides the freedom to risk, with courage, new horizons rather than focusing on limitations. The hope that grows out of basic trust, which Joan Erikson describes, also encourages older people to take risks, even as they detach themselves from material possessions and seek solitude.

Which brings greater contentment and happiness: lives like Bob's that are filled with intellectual pursuits and physical exercise? Or more passive time spent in reflection? The answer for a majority of older people lies in a combination of the two. Sometimes passivity needs to be challenged, as long as the need for silence and reflection is honored.

Final Thoughts

Spiritual journeys are often traveled in the space between being and doing. As people live into the social worlds of family, work, community, and society, they become absorbed in their roles and "lose sight of the liberating 'qualities of being' that are there also."[54] A spiritual life brings *being* back into their consciousness and helps them see the spiritual terrain of life more clearly. "If we want to understand how the spiritual region of life interacts with aging, we need a good map of the spiritual region," says Atchley. And probably a little help from friends, family, and a community of faith.

Reflection Questions

* If no one phase of life is more important than another, why do we resist so strongly the idea of growing old?

* Sara Lawrence-Lightfoot says, "The developmental terrain grows more layered; patience trumps speed; restraint trumps ambition; wisdom trumps IQ; 'leaving a legacy' trumps 'making our mark'; and a bit of humor saves us all." Are you more concerned about making a mark or leaving a legacy?

* "People tell us they are different people at eighty. They have new interests, and they have left some things behind." Does introspection excite or scare you? What are key moments or events in your life that you didn't have time to deal with? Can you find time now to go back and deal with the emotions, regrets, joys, or sorrows associated with those moments or events?

* Robert Atchley believes that spiritual journeys are often traveled in the space between being and doing. How could you effectively balance the two in your life?

Notes

1. Richard P. Johnson, "Shaping a New Vision of Faith Formation for Maturing Adults: Sixteen Fundamental Tasks," *Lifelong Faith*, Spring 2007, accessed December 27, 2017, http://www.faithformationlearningexchange.net/uploads /5/2/4/6/5246709/faith_formation_for_maturing_adults_-_johnson.pdf.

2. Susan Jacoby, *Never Say Die: The Myth and Marketing of the New Old Age* (New York: Pantheon Books, 2011), 11-12.

3. Barbara Klammerlohr, "Barbara's Room: Book Reviews and Article," Spring 2009, accessed December 27, 2017, http://www.secondjourney.org/kammerlohr /09Spr.htm.

4. Adele Hayutin, Miranda Dietz, and Lillian Mitchell, "New Realities of an Older America: Challenges, Changes and Questions," Stanford Center on Longevity, 2010, accessed December 27, 2017, http://longevity.stanford.edu /blog/2010/11/19/new-realities.

5. Sara Lawrence-Lightfoot, *The Third Chapter* (New York: Sarah Crichton Books, 2009), 173.

6. Peter Francese, "The MetLife Report of Early Boomers," MetLife Mature Market Institute, 2010, accessed December 27, 2017, https://www.metlife.com/assets /cao/mmi/publications/studies/2010/mmi-early-boomers.pdf.

7. Charles A. Cefalu, "Theories and Mechanisms of Aging," *Clinics in Geriatric Medicine* 27 (2011): 491-506, doi:10.1016/j.cger.2011.07.001.

8. Ibid., 498-500.

9. Milton Crum, *I'm Old*, monograph, 2011, accessed March 16, 2018, https://vts .myschoolapp.com/ftpimages/95/download/Milton%20Crum%20I%20 AM%20OLD%202011[4]_resources.pdf, 13-14.

10. Milton Crum, *I'm Frail*, monograph, 2014, accessed March 16, 2018, http:// www.ahpcc.org.uk/wp-content/uploads/2013/04/imfrail.pdf, 3.

11. Centers for Disease Control and Prevention website, "Healthy Aging," January 31, 2017, accessed December 27, 2017, https://www.cdc.gov/aging/mentalhealth /depression.htm.

12. Ibid.

13. Center for Behavioral Health Statistics and Quality, *Behavioral Health Trends in the United States: Results from the 2014 National Survey on Drug Use and Health*, 2015 (HHS Publication no. SMA 15-4927, NSDUH Series H-50), accessed November 18, 2017, retrieved from http://www.samhsa.gov/data.

14. Ibid.

15. The Henry J. Kaiser Family Foundation, "Total Number of Retail Prescription Drugs Filled at Pharmacies by Payer" (2016), accessed December 27, 2017, https://www.kff.org/health-costs/state-indicator/total-retail-rx-drugs/.

16. Harry Haroutunian, *Not as Prescribed: Recognizing and Facing Alcohol and Drug Misuse in Older Adults* (Center City, MN: Hazelden Publishing, 2016), 5.

17. Elaine M. Brody, "On Being Very, Very Old: An Insider's Perspective," *The Gerontologist* 50, no. 1 (February 2010): 2-10, doi.org/10.1093/geront/gnp143.

18. Ibid., 5.

19. Shanker Vedantam, "Older Americans May be Happier than Younger Ones," *Washington Post*, July 14, 2008, A04.

20. *State of American Well-Being: State Well-Being Rankings for Older Americans.* Gallup-Healthway Well-Being Index, 2015, accessed December 27, 2017, http://www.well-beingindex.com/hubfs/Well-Being_Index/2014_Data /Gallup-Healthways_State_of_American_Well-Being_Older_Americans _Rankings.pdf?t=1508795566327, 2.

21. Ibid.

22. The General Social Surveys, 1972–2016, National Opinion Center (NORC) at the University of Chicago, 2017, accessed December 27, 2017, http://gss.norc .org.

23. Catherine E. Ross and John Mirowsky, "Age and the Balance of Emotions," *Social Science and Medicine* 66 (2008): 2391-2400, doi:10.1016/j.socsci med.2008.01.048.

24. Donald F. Clingan, "Foreword: What Spiritual Well-Being Means to Me," in *Perspectives on Spiritual Well-Being and Aging,* ed. James A. Thorson (Springfield, IL: Charles C. Thomas, 2000), xiii.

25. Robert Atchley, *Spirituality and Aging* (Baltimore: The Johns Hopkins University Press, 2009), 2.

26. Ibid., 2-3.

27. C. Bruce Davis, "Spirituality and Aging," in *Perspectives on Spiritual Well-Being and Aging*, 45.

28. Ibid.

29. Richard Rohr, *Falling Upward* (New York: Jossey-Bass, 2011), xiii, 1.

30. Robert N. Butler, "The Life Review: An Interpretation of Reminiscence in the Aged," *Psychiatry* 26 (1963): 65-76, published online November 7, 2016, accessed December 1, 2017, doi.org/10.1080/00332747.1963.11023339.

31. James A. Thorson, ed., *Perspectives on Spiritual Well-Being and Aging* (Springfield, IL: Charles C. Thomas Publisher, 2000), xvi.

32. Bruce Stevens, *Hidden Learning: The Way We Are Wired for Intimacy* (Freemantle, Western Australia: Vivid Publishing, 2017), 6.

33. Ibid.

34. Ibid., 9.

35. Bruce A. Stevens, "The Life Tasks Model: Enhancing Psychological and Spiritual Growth in the Aged," *Journal of Religion, Spirituality & Aging* 29, September 7,

2017 (online), accessed November 10, 2017, http://dx.doi.org/10.1080/15528 030.2017.1365040.

36. Ibid.
37. Erik Erikson, *Identity and the Life Cycle* (New York: W. W. Norton & Company, 1997), 98.
38. Erik Erikson, *The Life Cycle Completed*, extended version (New York: W. W. Norton & Company, 1997), 112.
39. Ibid., 113; Erik Erikson, *Childhood and Society* (New York: W. W. Norton & Company, 1963), 269.
40. Erikson, *Life Cycle Completed*, 113.
41. Ibid.
42. "12 Requests from Someone with Alzheimer's," The Center for Aging Alzheimer's Family Support Program at Duke University Medical Center, accessed November 16, 2012, http://www.dukefamilysupport.org.
43. Donald Capps, *The Decades of Life: A Guide to Human Development* (Louisville, KY: Westminster John Knox Press, 2008), 175.
44. Ibid., 169.
45. Ibid., 159.
46. Lars Tornstam, "Gero-transcendence: A Reformulation of the Disengagement Theory," *Aging* 1 (1989): 55-63.
47. Froma Walsh, "Families in Later Life: Challenges and Opportunities," in *The Changing Family Life Cycle,* 2nd ed., ed. Betty Carter and Monica McGoldrick (Boston: Allyn and Bacon, 1989), 307-326.
48. Lars Tornstam, "Maturing into Gerotranscendence," *Journal of Transpersonal Psychology* 43, no. 2 (2011): 166-180, accessed December 27, 2017, http:// www.atpweb.org/jtparchive/trps-43-11-02-166.pdf, 167.
49. Ibid., 166-170.
50. Paula Span, "Aging's Misunderstood Virtues," *New York Times* blog, August 30, 2010, accessed December 27, 2017, https://newoldage.blogs.nytimes.com/2010 /08/30/appreciating-the-peculiar-virtues-of-old-age/.
51. Ibid.
52. K. Brynolf Lyon, "Faith and Development in Late Adulthood," in *Human Development and Faith,* 2nd ed., ed. Felicity B. Kelcourse (St. Louis: Chalice Press, 2015), 276.
53. Walsh, 320.
54. Atchley, 7.

CHAPTER 6

Embracing People Who Have Dementia

Before a church begins designing new Christian formation programs or selecting curriculum, it needs to identify its unique characteristics based on members of the congregation, and its location, history, and beliefs. Every church is different. When planning strategies for welcoming people with dementia and their caregivers into a worshiping community, churches need to take those same characteristics into account.

This chapter will address several issues in order to help congregations welcome people with dementia and honor the gifts these people bring with them. We begin by looking at the secrecy and myths that often accompany diseases like dementia and how to break down the barriers that separate us. We continue to cite theology to help congregations clarify their beliefs about God's relationship to different kinds of people and what that means for communities of faith. A section about communications will hopefully ease the integration of people with dementia into the life of a congregation. And finally, we widen our focus with the use of memory boxes to access the spiritual stories of people of all ages in a congregation.

Breaking Down Barriers of Secrecy

In just about any setting, when someone asks, "How are you?" the answer is most often a quick, "Fine." This is as true in houses of worship as in other places. We mask our problems, illnesses, worries, and concerns behind a meaningless word, unsure if the question is sincere or a social nicety. How does a community break down this façade to respond to people's lives with compassion and care?

The onset of dementia can be slow and difficult to detect, and family and caregivers may be reluctant to share the information with others. Unlike other illnesses, there is a stigma around a diagnosis of Alzheimer's or a related disease. Even though help may be desperately needed, many won't ask for it—even those who are long-term members of a congregation. A faith community, however, can be the best source of help and support.

✳ ✳ ✳

My dad could never bring himself to tell anyone that his wife had Alzheimer's. For a long time, I think he believed that if he didn't acknowledge her increasing forgetfulness and disorientation, maybe she would suddenly go back to her old self. Even surrounded by old friends, he simply couldn't say the words.

Church was a part of their normal routine, and they rarely missed going on Sunday. The regulars, especially those who had shared the same Sunday school class for over thirty years, knew that dad was struggling to keep up appearances as mom's caregiver. The women in the class decided they would take matters into their own hands.

When mom and dad arrived at their class on Sunday mornings, one of their longtime friends would approach. As she slid her arm around mom's waist, she dismissed dad to his duties as class treasurer. The role of being mom's companion for the morning rotated among the women in the class, but the actions were almost always the same. Watching this from the sidelines, I had a sense that mom was able to connect with these old friends through memories of familiarity.

Mom's smile never left her throughout her illness, and that was her gift in the transaction. Her friends would walk with her when she began to ramble around the room, always with a firm arm around her.

This group of people treated both Mom and Dad with respect and love, adding humor to smooth over any rough spots. They showed me through their gentle actions how a community could ease with Christian love the transitions we all face in life.—*Dorothy*

✳ ✳ ✳

Similar to the way the culture lumps everyone over sixty-five as "old," people with dementia are thrown into one category as well. While some of the differences among people with dementia may be nuanced and difficult to detect, those with mild or moderate dementia are far different from those with, for example, late-stage Alzheimer's disease. The participation and continued leadership of those with dementia in a congregation can result in added value to both their lives and those of others.

Dementia Myths

Katie Norris in a 2017 teleconference identified three myths related to congregational life that stymie the full inclusion of people with dementia. The first myth is that people with dementia can no longer serve in leadership roles. If the environment in which they serve is prepared with care, there is no reason to deny them an opportunity to use their gifts, Norris says.[1] She stresses the importance of talking directly to people with dementia about roles they might fill to let them know that they are still valued and a part of the community.

The second myth is the belief that people with dementia are disruptive. Perhaps we need to be as welcoming to this group as we are to others, such as families with young children. People with dementia often have shorter attention spans and prefer walking to sitting. A designated place for them to walk within gathering spaces of a church not only is welcoming to them and their caregivers, but also is less distracting for other worshipers.

✳ ✳ ✳

A clergy member told me about a person with dementia who would shout a random remark at some point during worship. This person preferred to sit near the front, where he had always sat. When he shouted, a member of the usher team was always ready to touch him lightly on the shoulder and slide into the pew next to him, where both remained in silence for the duration of the service. The congregation took his outbursts in stride, loving him rather than letting the episodes separate him from their presence.—*Dorothy*

* * *

The third myth is that the person with dementia won't remember other worshipers at services or events such as coffee hour. An argument could be made that many people *without* dementia don't recognize other members, especially at churches with multiple services. Social contact is the primary factor, not the ability to put a name to every face. Norris says that the person with dementia may not recognize some people, but they do remember the emotional relationship they have with them.[2]

* * *

A friend's mother who had moderate dementia joined a church bridge group soon after she moved in with her daughter. A strong player even with her memory loss, she became a valued member of the group. Although she could no longer drive, one of the group would always offer to take her home after their spirited games. When her dementia became more pronounced, she could no longer keep mental tabs of the cards that had been played. Her presence was still important to the group, even as her prowess in playing bridge declined. They faithfully kept tabs on her.

When her children decided to move her from the East Coast to California where most of them lived, the departure was celebrated with a party. The church bridge group all showed up to say goodbye. Even though she could not call them by name, the emotion of their relationship remained. They were friends whose relationship was built on silence sprinkled with laughter and stories. Dementia did not diminish their friendship even though it changed their relationship.—*Dorothy*

* * *

An Insider View

In the preface, we introduced Christine Bryden of Australia, who has had dementia for over twenty years. Church remains a mainstay in her life. She talks easily about her faith and certainty that God is an active player in it. She tells her audiences firmly that despite her dementia, "I am still Christine, loved by God, who can reflect on the unfolding narrative of her lived experience. . . . Vital to my continuing sense of being an embodied self is relating to God, which is not dependent on my cognitive abilities, my spiritual experiences, or my ability to talk about these. I relate to God in the stillness of muddled thoughts, with a sense of timelessness, where "there is only one safe place: 'here' with God."[3]

Bryden tells us that she is certain she experiences God's love, even if she is no longer able to express that experience clearly. "My inability to describe my experiences of God does not mean that I do not have them, which underscores the importance of an insider's view." Dementia does not separate her from God or the church community, although the narrative of meaning most often resides in the present moment rather than in the past or future. "I trust God to hold to all that I am, have ever been, and will ever be," she says.[4]

"I can be included within the faith community as an equal before God, which is the good news of the Gospel for those of us living with dementia. My worth is determined in God's eyes, who looks to my heart, not to what I can do or say," says Bryden. She strongly believes that God loves people equally as part of the richness and diversity of creation. "Even if I am less able to participate as part of the life of the worshipping community," she adds, "God sees me as a witness to what it means to be human: a recipient of divine love and grace."[5]

As an advocate for those living with dementia, she reminds us, "I am not my dementia. I am who I am before God in communion with others in my faith community. I am held in grace to the Father, through the Son, and by the Holy Spirit."[6]

Understanding Our Beliefs about Dementia

Theologian John Swinton has spoken about welcoming people with disabilities into communities and congregations despite their segregation in nursing homes and institutions. We should take issue in our churches with that kind of segregation, he said, instead of allowing "the most horrible things to become normal. We do that all the time in our culture. I think what churches need to do is become critically aware and think beyond the normal. Have a real look around and see whether some of the practices toward people are faithful to the traditions we come from."[7]

Congregations don't need to change who or what they are in order to expand their reach among those they serve. Swinton makes three important points about welcoming people with dementia. Begin by educating clergy about different disabilities, including dementia. "For the most part, clergy are not trained," he says. "They come to the parish situation with the same assumptions and expectations as the rest of society—that disability needs to be fixed—rather than asking, 'What does it mean to have [a disability] or advanced dementia and be a disciple?' "[8]

Secondly, "what you don't really need [are] special skills. Often, I hear congregations saying things like, 'We don't have the skills to look after these kinds of people.' But what skills would you need?"[9] The primary skill you need, he argues, is finding the time to be with someone and developing a relationship with them.

In our culture, both inside and outside the Church, there is an emphasis on inclusion that Swinton feels is "quite right" and points to his third observation. Inclusion is an appropriate starting point, but it is simply not enough. He says too often we include people in society just to have them there. "All we have to do is make the church [physically] accessible, have the right political structures, make sure people have a cup of tea at the end of the service or whatever."[10] Inclusion is only a beginning because of the chasm between inclusion and belonging. "To belong," he says, "you have to be missed. There's something really, really important about that. People need to long for you, to want you to be there. When you're not there, they should go looking for you."[11]

A primary goal of all communities, particularly religious communities, is providing a sense of belonging. The legal community can develop structures to protect people with disabilities and improve their lives, but it falls short in making people care for one another. "That seems to be a primary thing religious communities can do: create spaces where people can learn to care for one another, even if people are quite different. . . . And it's not just for people with disabilities or people with dementia. It's for all of us; we need to be missed."[12]

Bryden agrees with Kelsey and Swinton that being in relationship is an integral part of being human. "I cannot lose my membership in humanity, nor my ability to relate to God, simply by losing my neurones," Bryden says. "I can still express my spirituality within the faith community, where we all are dependent upon God."[13]

Swinton says that his research, which included his spending a great deal of time with people with disabilities and dementia, has helped him realize that "people are people, and that to be human is to be loved. It's not to have capacities, it's not to do or not do something; it's to be able to be loved." Being disabled or having dementia is simply another way of being human, he says. After you develop a relationship with a person with disabilities, you realize he or she is no different from yourself. "You get rid of the term 'people with disabilities' and just talk about people."[14]

Communications

Talking to and being with a person who has dementia is really no different than any other relationship. Some people may feel that they have to be responsible for two sides of a conversation when talking to a person with memory loss. They fill the silence with questions they answer themselves, as if memory loss also takes away speech and the ability to respond from the person with dementia. Conversations may need to slow down, but they can still exist. As in any relationship, listening is often more important than speaking.

Gerontologist Elaine Brody wrote in her research projects about the importance of listening:

> Many years ago, in a study of older people's day-to-day health concerns, we debriefed the interviewers and asked them, "What is the main piece of advice you can give health professionals?" The interviewers, over and over again, said, "Listen to what older people are really saying . . . not only to the words but to cries, whispers and silences. Really listen so that they know their concerns and feelings are being recognized."[15]

Her insight is as relevant for people with dementia as for other older people without it. Sometimes the *effort* of listening is more important than the spoken words that are shared.

There is evidence that our deepest memories survive despite diseases causing dementia. In chapter 5 we alluded to the tendency of older people to slip into old memories, which Robert Butler called "life review."[16] It is reasonable to assume that Butler's observations about the return to past experiences and unresolved conflicts could also occur in people with dementia. In fact, some, especially those in early stages of the disease, might find it easier to enter into a life review because they have already encountered their personal vulnerability as a result of their diminished capacities.

Building on Butler's ideas, James Thorson argues that there are significant benefits to encouraging elders to talk about their lives, and "just sitting still to listen to them is *grace*. We don't ask for it, we certainly don't deserve it, but it is freely given and it's what makes our lives worth living. Explaining ourselves," Thorson writes, "and finding that we are pretty good people after all is like forgiveness of sin; acceptance as we are is what we strive for and is what I think gives meaning to life."[17] Perhaps this kind of listening is the most important thing we can do with and for older people, even those who have dementia.

Talking and listening to a person with dementia may seem unnatural at first for some people, but there are ways to make communications work for both sides of a conversation. Katie Norris suggests that those initiating a conversation not feel pressured by unreasonable standards. Look around and find something in your setting to talk about, she says. Find a topic that relates to something you remember about that person. Pull up a photo on your phone and ask him or her what he or she sees in it. And, she adds, it is okay to be uncomfortable.[18]

A member of the congregation who had dementia very much enjoyed going to coffee hour after the 8:00 worship service. She had been a longtime Episcopalian, and this time of fellowship resided deep in her memories. Her dementia had not affected her love of people and conversation. Drinking coffee and chatting was in her "muscle memory"; she could go through the motions almost without thinking.

What she couldn't do too well was answer direct questions about events in her recent past. She always managed a response, but it was general and sometimes not on point. People close to her soon realized that she needed clues to help her recall an event or at least stay on topic. Instead of asking an open question about her recent trip to California, for example, a friend might turn the question into a statement: "I understand you stayed with your daughter on your trip to California. Is she doing well?" Even if she didn't remember the trip, she could talk about her daughter. And her friend could patiently listen.—*Dorothy*

* * *

Improving communication skills, says the Family Caregiver Alliance, can make encounters less stressful and improve the quality of a relationship. Its "Caregiver's Guide to Understanding Dementia Behaviors" offers the following tips:

- Setting a positive mood for interaction begins by being aware of attitudes and body language. Speaking in a pleasant and respectful manner sets a positive mood and conveys feelings of affection.
- Keeping noise and distractions at a minimum helps both parties in a conversation. Eye contact is important for getting and holding a person's attention. That means both sides need to be at the same "level," either sitting or standing. As in any conversation among friends, keeping voice levels consistent is easier to understand.
- Speaking slowly, using simple words and sentences conveys information without adding layers of complexity. Repetition and rephrasing sentences gives the person with dementia time to process a question or statement. Using the names of people and places instead of pronouns alone adds clarity by tapping into longer-term memory.
- Avoiding open-ended questions or ones with too many choices lessens confusion. Questions with yes or no answers often work best.
- Listening with ears, eyes, and heart lets people with dementia "know their concerns and feelings are being recognized."[19] Patience is of utmost importance, as listeners strive to discover the meaning and feelings that underlie the words.
- Breaking down activities and tasks into a series of steps is less taxing on people with poor short-term memory. A gentle touch on an arm or back can guide a person without being obtrusive.

- Changing the topic or moving to a new location if a person becomes upset or agitated allows a conversation to continue and gives them a chance to recover.
- Responding with affection and reassurance when someone with dementia recalls things that never happened is more important than trying to convince them that they are wrong. Their alternate reality is completely real to them.
- Remembering the past can be soothing and affirming to someone with short-term memory loss. Historical events can sometimes be recalled with amazing accuracy and detail.
- Being able to laugh together strengthens any relationship, as long as the humor is not at the expense of anyone. Many people with dementia retain their social skills and their senses of humor.[20]

Swinton reflected on his years as chaplain:

I guess, looking back, that was exactly what I was doing when I was sitting with people with dementia: trying in my awkward, embarrassed, and wordless way to hold people in their identity and to show them that I cared and that I was listening with my ears, with my eyes and with my soul. . . . Holding, naming, remembering, and companioning allow us in some way to share in the sacrament of the present moment with those for whom time has begun to slow down and stand still.[21]

Integrating People with Dementia into Congregations

Starting a new ministry within a congregation is never easy. Finding and training volunteers among competing ministries may be difficult. However, as more and more of the general population ages, which is correlated to the increasing number of people with dementia, a ministry for those with dementia is critical. Perhaps a subgroup of a pastoral care committee or a Stephen Ministries[22] group might be willing to take on this ministry, assisted by training in communicating with people who have dementia.

In England, where "Dementia-Friendly" campaigns are part of the cultural fabric, some churches have opened their doors and hearts to people with dementia and their caregivers. Margaret Goodall and Gaynor Hammond have written extensively about ways that churches could embrace those with dementia. In addition to listening and affirmation, they remind us of the importance of keeping in touch with people who attend infrequently or not at all. They recommend the designation of one or more people as "church friends," who provide the kind of hospitality Dorothy's mother received from her Sunday school friends each week. If possible, this person would be trained to talk to family members about dementia and knowledgeable about community resources that are available.

Two suggestions that we explore in chapter 7 involve worship and fellowship sharing. Memory cafés are now operating in many cities in houses of worship or community centers to provide welcoming spaces for people with dementia to connect with old and new friends.[23]

Hammond also identifies specific church practices that are not always dementia-friendly, as well as regular programming that is inclusive of people with dementia and their families. She cautions congregations to remember that these endeavors are works in progress. "It will take on a life of its own, it will develop, and it will grow and continue to grow . . . the most difficult hurdle to overcome is the first one: getting started."[24] Hammond notes that the outward changes churches can make to be welcoming and inclusive, such as installing ramps, sound systems for the hearing-impaired, comfy seats, and even a friendly welcome at the door, are just starting points.

> Being a Dementia-Friendly Church is about looking for ways in which those who have dementia, along with their families and friends, can feel they are completely included as valued members of the congregation. . . . I would ensure that the person who has dementia, and their carer, would be cared for through all the stages of the illness . . . spiritually and pastorally supported and nurtured in order for them to enjoy being part of a worshipping community in every sense.[25]

Spiritual Autobiographies and Memory Boxes

Looking back at our spiritual lives can be an enriching experience for people of all ages. Mary Clark Moschella suggests that spiritual autobiography groups provide a pastoral ministry that can enrich the lives of older adults, their families, and their congregations. She writes that "the process of composing one's spiritual autobiography is often a life-giving activity . . . the telling or sharing of this story with others in a faith community can be particularly salutary, especially for older adults."[26]

Telling our life stories, writes Moschella, is a "brave and daring endeavor. It involves naming one's own reality, calling it something, just as God called 'worlds into being.' "[27] She warns that the perceived invisibility of many older people, especially older women, increases the difficulty of the task.

> When an older adult takes the action of telling or writing his or her story, a sense of strength or clarity may ensue. The very act of composing one's own story is an exercise of freedom that holds the potential to empower and enliven the author. . . . If the story that is shared is received or heard in a thoughtful and respectful manner, the person's feeling of clarity and well being will likely be magnified. There is blessed relief that comes from feeling understood, known, by another.[28]

She goes on to say that congregations often under-recognize and underuse the wisdom of older people. "While clergy and lay caregivers may recognize a duty to offer care *to* the elderly, rarely is the idea of ministry *with* older adults fully embraced or realized."[29] Using storytelling across generations, she believes, opens resources for spiritual growth for people of all ages.

Several years ago, a group of women in an ecumenical church planned a spring retreat about the spirituality of aging, specifically addressing their fears of the changes and losses of growing older. A member of the retreat planning committee had just been diagnosed with Alzheimer's disease, adding to their concerns. They asked Dorothy to be the retreat leader.

✳ ✳ ✳

Having just read Moschella's and others' descriptions of the power of spiritual autobiography, I planned to use it as the framework for the retreat. Former and current seminary students, however, were telling me that their attempts to encourage older people into storytelling through spiritual autobiography had failed, even in well-formed groups that had met for years. While people in these groups easily shared stories about their past, the idea of talking about the *spiritual* side of those experiences intimidated them.

About the same time, I began reading about the power of *memory boxes*, real boxes filled with memory cues for those who have dementia, including written stories, poetry, photos, music, scrapbooks, and other memorabilia. Influenced by the success of these boxes for a variety of people, I redirected my thoughts, still embracing the idea of spiritual autobiography but planning activities that focused on memory boxes. Participants brought box contents with them—photos, music, and stories—that we used during the retreat. The sessions were centered on the content they brought for their boxes that defined their identity and laid the groundwork for their stories. Each time we came together, we looked at scripture, statistics, and theory to give us a better understanding of aging, the meaning of spirituality, and how God's presence is a part of our journey. Against that backdrop, the group explored their own thoughts and fears about aging while tapping into their memories.—*Dorothy*

Although the group focused on photos, music, and stories for their boxes, some participants added other mementos as well. One brought an old skate key hanging on a string, an essential tool for tightening skates on hard-soled shoes. It reminded the group of the joy of skating and the freedom skates gave them to explore the boundaries of their neighborhoods. Others shared photos that elicited stories, often accompanied with peals of laughter, a tender smile, or even a tear. The group was gently reminded that their memories were a part of their lives, companions on their journeys.

*   *   *

I learned about memory boxes too late for mom and dad. But they both, and especially dad, taught me how memories can bring a moment of joy or a flash of contentment that benefitted us all. When I realized that I needed to move dad closer to my home, I began looking for mementos in the house that he had lived in for over fifty years. I worried about uprooting him from familiar surroundings and hoped that I could identify items that would be comforting. He was born in Oklahoma and had spent all of his life there, except during his deployment during World War II. My husband used to say that if you pricked his finger, my dad would bleed Oklahoma.

I carefully packed up plaques and certificates honoring the work he did as president of his accounting association and at his church, where he was a deacon emeritus. I brought the covered cookie bowl he had used for over thirty years, which I remember as never being empty. The scrapbook he had compiled about his World War II experiences I carried on the plane with us, not trusting moving companies or the mail. I found pictures and keepsakes of his fifty-plus years' marriage to my mother, including their courtship on an air base in southern Oklahoma. Almost as an afterthought, I threw in a class photo from his grade school in Waukomis and a skunk trap he had used as a boy to earn extra spending money. I filled his apartment in an assisted living facility with the items that I brought from his home. I hung the plaques and certificates, prominently displayed photos of him with my mother, filled the cookie jar with his favorite cookies, displayed his WWII scrapbook, and stocked a small refrigerator with items I knew he enjoyed.

Soon I realized that the plaques and certificates were part of a past he simply did not remember. His memories of my mother folded into my ongoing presence where wife/daughter became a single person in his mind. The cookies (similar to items in the refrigerator) were never eaten: out of sight, out of mind. The mementos that sparked conversations between us were his WWII scrapbook, the class photo, which was unframed and slightly beaten-up, the skunk trap, and my unreliable memory of stories he had told us about growing up on a farm. He could tell me the names of every single person in the photo—about twenty-five in all. He remembered Christmas dinner on the barren island off Africa where he was stationed during the war. And I only had to start a childhood story about his cousins, and he would finish it.

I have often wondered what he would have included in a memory box before his dementia became prominent. Maybe he would have focused on the latter part of his life as I had. But our experience together has made me reach back to my earliest memories as I continue to add items to my own box.—*Dorothy*

* * *

Because wisdom and experience are not necessarily destroyed by brain disease, people with dementia can participate in recalling memories and in the storytelling that Moschella says "can promote interchange and interpersonal connection between members of different generations."[30] Even if stories come from an alternate reality and are not always grounded in a present reality, they can still reflect the experience and wisdom gained from life and subsequent reflection.

The power of memory boxes is not limited to people who have dementia or even older adults. Although memories can at times be devastating, they also have the power to heal people of all ages. Curating the contents of memory boxes over time helps people remember their stories and mark their spiritual growth.

✳ ✳ ✳

When Hurricane Harvey hit Houston, Roger thought his family would be able to ride out the storm in their home. He and his wife, Kristin, and teenage daughter, Riley, had recently moved to the area from their longtime home in South Carolina. As the rains continued to pound the region, they realized they needed to move to higher ground. They grabbed a few items, including Scout, their pet dog, and drove to the home of new friends, a safe haven amid the destruction that surrounded them. Roger described on Facebook what happened later that night:

"Dad. Look what I packed!" Our almost-grown woman-child Riley stands in the doorway with a lidded box—about the size of a shoebox. "It's my memory box. I started filling it up a long time ago . . . and I kept filling it. I didn't want to leave it. You want to look at it with me?" She looked like the three-year-old I remember and the twenty-seven-year-old that I can't wait to hang out with.

So we did . . . right there on the floor of someone else's home, a home that has become our safe place for now. There were photos, postcards, Adele tickets, letters, and more. She told me about every one of them. For a brief moment we were transported back in time, far away from falling rain and worry. I am so proud of Kristin and Riley. Scout is pretty awesome, too. We are family and we are going to be okay. I know I will have a few things to add to my "memory box."
—Roger Hutchison[31]

✳ ✳ ✳

Whether stories are told within families or in more formal spiritual autobiography groups at a church, among all age groups or targeted to older people, including those with dementia, it is the sharing of stories that enriches lives. Moschella suggests that stories be spoken aloud in worship or other congregational gatherings, or recorded and written for family and/or church archives. Sharing stories, she says, could lead to rich theological conversations through which people reflect upon their values and beliefs. She writes:

> Listening to the life stories of older adults is indeed an act of love, one that can enrich the lives of congregants of all ages. Story listening can reveal the spiritual dimensions of elders' lives that often go untapped or even unnamed. . . . Questions that get at issues of values, transcendence, hope, or despair can bring forth the kind of stories that matter most, to both teller and listener. Such stories are worth telling, hearing, and remembering in communities of faith.[32]

Full Circle

This chapter returns us again to the concept of how God extends grace and love to all people, wherever they are in life. We rediscover that it is in our relationships with each other that we *experience* that love. We may need to learn a few new skills to help us communicate with some who have dementia. We may need to listen more intently to hear what older people are saying, "not only to the words, but to cries, whispers, and silences. Really listen so that they know their concerns and feelings are being recognized."[33] We may need to rely on cues from boxes of mementos to ask the right questions to elicit memories from long ago. It is in these redeeming actions that we find redemption ourselves.

Reflection Questions

✳ Have you been guided by any of the three myths that Katie Norris identified? How could you address these myths in your congregation?

✳ John Swinton said, "To belong, you have to be missed." Do you agree? How does your faith community respond if a member goes "missing"?

✳ Do we sometimes overlook people with dementia because of their lack of cognitive skills? How does Christine Bryden, who has had dementia for twenty years, respond to her sense of self?

✳ Which tips about listening to and talking with people with dementia did you find most helpful?

✳ Which of your mementos, photos, or music would be most useful in remembering the past? Would you be interested in creating your own memory box?

✳ How could your congregation incorporate storytelling into its programming?

Notes

1. Katie Norris, "Creating Dementia Friendly Congregations," teleconference, May 30, 2017, accessed December 3, 2017, https://www.revkatienorris.com/workshops.
2. Ibid.
3. Christine Bryden and Elizabeth MacKinlay, "Dementia—a Spiritual Journey Towards the Divine: A Personal View of Dementia," in *Mental Health and Spirituality in Later Life*, ed. Elizabeth MacKinlay (New York: Haworth Pastoral Press, 2002), 11.
4. Ibid., 10.
5. Christine Bryden, "A Continuing Sense of Self Within the Lived Experience of Dementia," presenation at the Seventh International Conference on Ageing and Spirituality, June 4-7, 2017, Chicago, Illinois, accessed June 16, 2017, www.7thinternationalconference.org.
6. Ibid.
7. Chelsea Temple Jones, "Interview with John Swinton," *UCObserver,* February 2013, accessed November 28, 2017, http://www.ucobserver.org/interviews/2013/02/john_swinton/.
8. Ibid.
9. Ibid.
10. Ibid.
11. Ibid.
12. Ibid.
13. Bryden, "A Continuing Sense of Self."
14. Jones, "Interview with John Swinton."
15. Elaine M. Brody, *Mental and Physical Health Practices of Older People* (New York: Springer Publishing, 1985), quoted in Elaine M. Brody, "On Being Very,

Very Old: An Insider's Perspective," *The Gerontologist* 50, no. 1 (2010): accessed December 4, 2017, https://doi.org/10.1093/geront/gnp143.

16. Robert N. Butler, "The Life Review: An Interpretation of Reminiscence in the Aged," *Psychiatry* 26 (1963): 65-76, published online November 7, 2016, accessed December 1, 2017, https://doi.org/10.1080/00332747.1963.110233 39.

17. James Thorson, ed., *Perspectives on Spiritual Well-Being and Aging* (Springfield, IL: Charles C. Thomas Publisher, LTD, 2000), xvi.

18. Norris, "Creating Dementia Friendly Congregations."

19. Brody, *Mental and Physical Health Practices*, 9.

20. "Caregiver's Guide to Understanding Dementia Behaviors," Family Caregiver Alliance, National Center on Caregiving, accessed November 17, 2017, https://www.caregiver.org/caregivers-guide-understanding-dementia-behaviors.

21. John Swinton, *Dementia: Living in the Memories of God* (Grand Rapids, MI: William B. Eerdmans Publishing Company, 2012), 242.

22. https://www.stephenministries.org/

23. Margaret Goodall and Gaynor Hammond, *Growing Dementia-Friendly Churches: A Practical Guide* (Great Britain: Methodist Homes Association and Christians on Aging [CCOA], 2013): 15-18, accessed December 4, 2017, http://www.mha.org.uk/files/3814/0931/8295/Growing_Dementia_Friendly _Churches.pdf.

24. Gaynor Hammond, *Growing Dementia-Friendly Churches* (Great Britain: Methodist Homes Association and Christians on Aging [CCOA], 2015), 6.

25. Ibid.

26. Mary Clark Moschella, "Spiritual Autobiography and Older Adults," *Journal of Pastoral Psychology* 60 (2011): 95-96.

27. Ibid., 96.

28. Ibid.

29. Ibid., 97.

30. Ibid.

31. Roger Hutchison, August 2017, shared with permission.

32. Moschella, "Spiritual Autobiography," 98.

33. Brody, *Mental and Physical Health Practices*, 9.

CHAPTER 7

Serving with People Who Have Dementia

As brain diseases such as Alzheimer's progress, people with dementia respond differently. Some prefer the rhythms and repetition of familiar traditions of family, friends, and faith communities. Others experiencing shorter attention spans, loss of language skills, and other disease-related complications prefer new settings created with their needs in mind, such as special worship services and Memory Cafés. Many gravitate to both kinds of events, perhaps attending a regular worship service on Sunday morning with a caregiver and also dropping into a Memory Café later in the week.

Whether planning a weekly social gathering or a monthly worship service for people with dementia, or working with ushers at regularly scheduled services to accommodate physical needs for access, the desires and opinions of those with dementia add important guidance. When planning an event or program *for* a group, it is easy to insert our own biases. When we plan *with* representation from that group, we are more likely to consider different ideas that are more consistent with the needs of the people we serve.

In this chapter, we will look at different ways people with dementia can worship at houses of worship, special facilities, or at home. We describe Memory Cafés, social gathering sites that are springing up all over the country, and coordinated pastoral care for those who are ill, frail, or have dementia.

Opportunities to serve others continue to provide meaning and purpose throughout people's lives even if they have a disability such as dementia. The chapter ends with a discussion of the importance of advocacy for increased research initiatives, appropriate care for those with dementia, and ongoing support for their caregivers.

Worship

Community worship is the central focus of faith for many religions. The rhythms of liturgy draw us in with insights from the present and reflections from the past. The repetition of prayers, scripture, music, and creeds breeds a familiarity that even the encroachment of time and dementia can't destroy. Including people with dementia into regular worship is always appropriate. We noted in chapter 6 the importance of Christian community to Christine Bryden, who has lived with dementia for over twenty years. She said:

> I have reflected on the role of my faith community, and how important it is for people with dementia to be enfolded within worship in community, rather than as individuals. I propose that we need to think of church as a "We-Thou" communion in which we are all enfolded in worship as a community before God. I am part of the Body of Christ and can partake in all acts of remembrance, despite my failing memory, and of worship, despite my failing understanding.[1]

She says the sacramental act of the Eucharist continually gives her a glimpse of wonder. "This is important to me in my struggles with perceptions of time and with memory loss, and is a sacred moment in worship that particularly resonates with me."[2]

Worshiping at Regularly Scheduled Services

Accommodations for people at worship services who are at differing stages of dementia can be made with little disruption. Ushers can be prepared to offer appropriate seating and to provide assistance during communion. Trained greeters might sit next to or near a person with dementia or be ready to accompany them if they get distracted and start to wander. What we need to remember is how this sacred time and place resonates with older people who may or may not have dementia. Anne Karoly recalls the reactions of her mother, who at eighty-seven has dementia, to the worship service they attended each week.

※ ※ ※

The liturgy is so ingrained she can still recite prayers and responses, even as other memories recede. She listens attentively during the sermon, even though none of the words will stick. She pesters me until our check is deposited in the plate. At communion, she offers thanksgiving while consuming the bread and wine. Sunday worship still is central to her life. She's been all-in since she was a babe in her mother's arms. And even now, as her memories slip into a dementia-induced fog, she retains a firm grasp on her Episcopal identity.[3]
—Anne Karoly

※ ※ ※

Worshiping at Specially Designed Services

There comes a time for some in the late stages of dementia when regular worship services are no longer desirable. Perhaps they came to faith later in life, and the words that resonate with others are lost in brains that no longer access more recent information. Others may live in nursing homes or assisted living communities where worship is irregular or from a tradition that seems foreign.

Congregations can collaborate with other faith communities in the area to offer specialized worship services for people with dementia and their caregivers. Special services can also be a part of regular worship at retirement communities and nursing homes. Those who have worked with other populations with special needs have developed good resources for planning and preparing worship services. *Rhythms of Grace*, for example, provides helpful tips in planning worship services for children with short attention spans.[4] Whenever resources designed for other targeted audiences are adapted for older people, they should take into account adults' different life experiences. Successful worship services will tap into elders' experiences and their memories of traditions, liturgies, and music.

Echoing Nancey Murphy, Bryden reminds us that we can learn from the practices of the ancient Hebrews, who experienced personal identity in community. "Worship acceptable in God's sight," she said, "emanated from the collective lives of the people." Parts of our worship, she adds, such as the Lord's Prayer and the Nicene Creed, both are communal statements that recognize "our sense of being a continuing embodied self in relationship with God and with others."[5]

Liturgist James W. Farwell would agree. The fundamental anthropological unity of liturgy is the assembly, he said, not the individual. Liturgy comprises the full range of our bodily participation that includes but is not simply the cognitive. "The assembly meets at the initiative of God who is first to re-member us. Our remembrance is our consent to God's initiative toward us, and our participation in it. We make that consent as a liturgical assembly." Farwell went on to say that "within the assembly, there is always a range of capacities, intentionality, and level of engagement. Those with dementia are no less qualified as individual members of that assembly than anyone else."[6] While the liturgy is based in part on words, it is ultimately beyond words, a fact that people with dementia can help us understand.

Drawing on these resources, the wisdom of chaplains at retirement communities and nursing homes, and our own experiences, we created a list of suggestions for creating separate worship services for people with dementia and their families and caregivers:

- Invite a group of people to create and direct regular worship experiences for people with dementia. Committee members might include people with dementia, caregivers, social workers, clergy, and a representative of a worship committee, among others. Including a person with dementia will add legitimacy to the committee's work and help it to identify issues that might otherwise be overlooked.
- Schedule worship services at a set time and place weekly, monthly, or quarterly to provide consistency. Services in retirement communities may be scheduled more often than those in churches, but going to a church facility may be important to some. Sacred space can be created anywhere, but the space for worship should be consistent and treated with the same reverence as other designated worship areas. Seating should be comfortable, keeping in mind the age of

many of the participants. Chairs with arms to support people when they sit or stand are helpful. Uncluttered aisles or areas where participants can walk allow them to be a part of the service even if they are moving around.

- Hospitality trumps almost all other considerations. Worshipers should be treated with respect, knowing that they have valid experiences with God, even if those experiences cannot be shared with words. They have something to teach us if we listen and spend time with them.

- Music is vital. It allows people of all ages and conditions to access their deepest core. If given the chance, participants often can name or sing their favorite hymns, spirituals, or praise music. Observation will provide the best insight into the kind of music a particular group prefers.

- Liturgies should be short and appropriate for the audience. For Episcopal Eucharist services, liturgist James W. Farwell suggests the "Order for Celebrating the Holy Eucharist" from the Book of Common Prayer[7] (see box on the next page). He believes that the inclusion of the basic components provides a worship experience appropriate for all people, whether they have dementia or not. He does not prescribe specific language for any of the components, although he suggests selecting words that are likely to be familiar to worshipers when possible. At the beginning of Eucharist service during the Easter season, for example, the celebrant says, "Alleluia. Christ is risen." The people respond, "The Lord is risen indeed. Alleluia." These responses often tap into people's deepest memories, even if they can no longer read, providing a deep contentment of being part of a community. In addition, says Farwell, the use of short sentences and simple language is completely acceptable.[8]

Worshiping in Homes

A third alternative for worship is at home, which allows older people "to experience the spiritual discipline of congregational worship, with the desired result of enabling them to find hope in God's faithful presence with them each day."[10] A "Church at Home" program is offered by a Baptist church in Atlanta for all people who find it difficult to attend regular worship at a church. This could easily be modified for people with dementia.

Components of an Episcopal Eucharist Service[9]
- Gather in God's name
- Hear and respond to the Word of God
- Pray for the world and the Church
- Exchange the Peace
- Prepare the altar
- Give thanks
  Structure of the Eucharistic Prayer: The Great Thanksgiving
  — *Sursum corda*: exchange of greetings
  — *Pre-Sanctus* or preface: thanksgiving for God the Creator
  — *Sanctus/Benedictus*: proclaiming the holiness of God
  — *Post-Sanctus*: praising God for the long arc of salvation history
  — *Words of Institution*: remembering the Last Supper
  — *Anamnesis/Oblation*: making the past present in the presence of the Risen One and offering the gifts and ourselves
  — *Acclamation*: praising God together
  — *Epiclesis*: petitioning the Holy Spirit to bless and transform the gathering
  — *Doxology/Amen*: summarizing the Trinity, followed by the "People's Amen"
- Break the bread
- Share the Body and Blood of Christ
- Be sent forth into the world

In Church at Home three to five people from the congregation, called encouragers, gather in the home of an isolated elder to share in congregational worship. . . . Each Church at Home gathering includes hymns, prayers, scripture reading, a sermon, and Communion. The congregational hymns are led by a confident singer, each sung unaccompanied or accompanied by a violin. Though the small group singing may not be as robust as in a large congregation, the familiar hymn tunes and texts retain their spiritual power.[11]

All of the participants in the program, including both encouragers and elders, have benefitted from the relationships that have been created.

"Wherever a church has older members or older neighbors in the community," write Sara Robb and Greg Smith, "there is a need and a ministry opportunity to serve as the presence of Christ in their lives."[12]

In reflecting on her parish ministry for children with autism, Audrey Scanlan realized that through worship experiences they had become a community. "We learned about each other's particular sensitivities, tastes, tolerances, and how to honor them." At first, she added, they worried at the end of each session about how much each participant had "gotten," and wondered if their work was "getting through." Then they stopped asking those questions.

> We learned to trust that the Spirit was at work in and through us, and we learned, over time, that not only had our new members been transformed, but that we had, too, in sighs too deep for words (Romans 8:26).[13]

Worship planned by and for people with dementia can have the same outcome, especially if leadership stops worrying if their message is "getting through" and starts living into God's work among everyone involved.

Memory Cafés

One of the challenges people with dementia face is isolation. They may not want to risk their safety and the embarrassment and awkwardness of getting lost or making mistakes. A person with early-stage dementia will often make excuses and decline invitations to social events even in close communities such as extended family and his or her congregation. In response, friends and extended family pull back, creating a real deficit in the person's life. This not only decreases the person's well-being through grief about the loss of family and friends, but also increases fear of the distancing friends, which gives rise to stigmatizing dementia.

In 1997, psychologist Bère M. L. Miesen of the Netherlands introduced Memory Cafés, which recognize the need for people with dementia and their caregivers to have places to socialize and be welcomed and supported by others in similar situations. "If you attend Alzheimer's Café sessions," he said, "you acknowledge that you have something to do with the disease. . . . That's a significant step for nearly everyone and is crucial to being able to live and cope with it. . . . I personally find it a sort of ritual for getting rid of your fear. We all know that tragedy is not deep and sharp if it can be shared with friends."[14]

The café is largely an informal get-together that provides a relaxing respite from an isolated care situation at home or from more clinical environments in facilities. Confidentiality is assured. Typical guests are people with dementia in various stages, along with their care partners, who may be spouses, children, grandchildren, friends, or professional caregivers. In Europe, Memory Cafés tend to have some structure that includes distributing information about illnesses causing dementia, care ideas, and resources. In the United States, the cafés are less structured and more like coffeehouses with relaxed atmospheres where participants can take a brief respite from dementia.

In churches, restaurants, community centers, libraries, and museums, Memory Cafés often provide light food and drink, and sometimes activities and entertainment. They are usually open once a month, but participants may visit more than one café if several are available in their area. The Memory Café is not a support group. A cadre of volunteers engages visitors, listening and encouraging meaningful, social interactions. Usually the central organizers have some experience in the field of dementia, and volunteers have basic training.

Taking my mother out for dinner was enjoyable, but eventually more challenging as the disease progressed. When I took her out to eat, we enjoyed the meals thoroughly, but we tended to make a mess of the table. I started taking mom to restaurants around 3:00 p.m. when they were emptier, so we wouldn't disturb others or deal with their stares. To avoid this kind of awkward situation, a Memory Café might have been a better option and would have had the benefit of providing company and support. I wish that Memory Cafés had existed in our community while my mother was still mobile. I would have greatly appreciated the company of others in my situation, and I think it would have been a great relief to my mom not to be the only one she knew with a memory disorder.—*Janice*

✳ ✳ ✳

According to participants, Memory Cafés increase feelings of hope and reduce feelings of isolation and loneliness caused by dementia. Social engagement is valued as simply an improvement in quality of life. At the Memory Café, people with dementia can meet others with similar concerns, make friends, and regain a sense of normalcy. They can talk about favorite movies, foods, hobbies, and share jokes. Sally Quinn described a conversation of men with dementia who met regularly:

> One man sat quietly, not participating at all. There were others in the group, the newer ones, who seemed quite normal until, after an hour or so, they began repeating themselves. Every once in a while, one of them would stop in the middle of talking and say, "I can't remember [anything]!" The others would totally crack up with appreciation.[15]

Caregivers can build bonds with others in similar situations for peer support and friendship. Many experience a renewal in their work from seeing it from another perspective, which is sometimes spiritual.

* * *

Sibley Hospital's Club Memory is one of the longest standing cafés in the Washington, DC, area, and its model is beginning to spread throughout the city. When I had the opportunity to visit, several people greeted me, and it was unclear to me who had dementia, who were caregivers, and who were serving as volunteers. Four tables were set up with different activities—singing, painting, playing cards, and one with a game called Mexican Train. I joined the latter table and was taught how to play by several people, who later told me they had dementia. I think they let me win the first game, and only by their providing a lot of help. I could feel the warmth, welcome, and camaraderie among participants. Judging by the laughter in the room, the groups clearly had a great deal of fun, and they were already talking about and looking forward to the next café.—*Janice*

* * *

With increasing memory loss and challenges in accomplishing daily tasks, social interactions can reduce stress, behavioral challenges, and some need for medications. Regular outings also may lengthen the time the person with dementia can remain at home.

Simple socialization has added benefits for everyone involved. Participants who have symptoms of dementia but have not gotten a formal diagnosis may seek the medical care they need by observing coping skills of those who have been diagnosed. Caregivers can observe how trained volunteers interact with those who have dementia and learn new skills for coping with a demanding nonstop job. Social networks may become deeper than the monthly gathering at a Memory Café, as participants befriend each other and exchange contact information. If the café reaches out to local businesses and other organizations for sponsorship or promotional partnership, it will further educate the community about the need for dementia awareness.

Having your church host a Memory Café is consistent with the mission of hospitality, allowing members to live their faith by caring for others. Many people trust churches as safe places. Activities at church-run Memory Cafés might include worship, Bible study, and hymn singing, providing a vital new resource for members who may have dementia, as well as for their families and caregivers. Neighbors may participate as well, extending the mission of the church. Volunteers, including students, become advocates for people with dementia. Rich or poor, black or brown or white, straight or gay, of differing faiths, nationalities, and cultures, dementia affects everyone. Inclusivity is a value of the Memory Café movement. Guidelines for starting a Memory Café are widely available, with a range of activities to match goals, budget, and scope.[16]

Pastoral Care Volunteers

One organization designed to train and support pastoral care volunteers is called Community of Hope International (COH). It prepares laypeople to provide pastoral care in different settings, from retirement communities to nursing homes and hospitals, from prisons and homeless ministries to churches and home visitations. Pastoral care is defined as "being 'present' in a listening, compassionate, non-controlling manner to an individual or groups for the purpose of consciously or unconsciously representing them and seeking to respond to their spiritual needs."[17]

Helen Appelberg started the program in Texas, from where it spread to over 125 centers in the United States, British Columbia, Canada, Mexico, and Malawi. Key to the program is a fourteen-module training that includes both theoretical and practical topics, ranging from the tenets of Benedictine spirituality to practical tips in making a pastoral care visit. The training is available at COH centers and online.

The unique component of this program is its emphasis on Benedictine spirituality. It emphasizes Jesus' call to care for the sick and the spiritual growth of each participant "because those who are the healthiest spiritually will have the most to give to others in need."[18] Volunteers in the program worship together, engage in continuing education and peer supervision, report and reflect on visitation information, and deepen their community ties through regular contact.

Maria Wellisch, a Community of Hope trainer for Morningside Ministries, a large senior living community in the San Antonio area, talked about ways Community of Hope removes barriers among residents. Spending time together has helped those living in independent housing be less wary of those in assisted living, and both groups discovered through their ministry new friendships with those in skilled nursing or memory care units.[19]

Before committing to Community of Hope, Wellisch looked at other pastoral care initiatives, such as Stephen Ministries. The one-on-one emphasis of Stephen Ministries was less appropriate for residents of her community, who often were frail and in hospice care. In Community of Hope where visitors often see several people each week, changes among people being visited were less difficult to manage.

Recently, a volunteer shared her diagnosis of Alzheimer's with others in her Community of Hope group, recalls Wellisch. Immediately the group rallied around her to look for ways she could still be fully involved as a visitor and member of the group. At that time, she could still read scripture passages for their regular worship, but was uncomfortable leading impromptu prayers. As the group continued to assess her strengths and weaknesses, they realized that others in the group needed the same kind of attention. Another volunteer in the group was losing her vision at a startling pace, but she was still able to listen to and reflect on the stories and observations of others. One person had slowly begun to rely on a wheelchair as his legs weakened. The group began to realize that almost all of them had some disability, but that together they could continue the pastoral care that had become such a part of their lives.[20]

Their response mirrors the concerns expressed by Benedict of Nursia, who wrote a "rule of life" for monks in sixth-century Italy to encourage them to seek God together in community. His rule is still observed around the world in monasteries and lay communities, such as Community of Hope, which was founded "to form praying communities, encouraging each other in love, to be a non-judgmental listening presence to those we encounter on a daily basis."[21] The founders of COH incorporated both humility and hospitality in the design of the program.

> The idea of hospitality—to see in each other the face of Christ—reminds us that we are all in this dance called "life" together, ultimately called to life in the Trinity. That is our destination, and we are to do everything we can to keep this in mind as we progress toward that end.[22]

People with dementia have greatly benefitted from communities and churches that offer a Community of Hope or similar pastoral care component. First-time pastoral visitors, who often are fearful about entering a memory unit to visit someone with dementia, discover the power of seeing Christ in the face of another, even if that "other" has dementia.

Vocations of Service for People with Dementia

Aging is usually associated with retirement, less activity, and more health concerns. But we all have anecdotal stories about the octogenarian who runs programs, elders who still shovel snow, or a ninety-something who still works in the church gift shop. Calendars of many older people are fuller now than they were before retirement, and vocations of service are still prominent. "If vocation is about God's call to persons (and communities) claiming us across the whole of our lives, surely God calls older adults to vocations of service and love too. But life and vocation in older adulthood are distinctive,"[23] writes theologian Joyce Ann Mercer.

Aging bodies are often the reason for the distinctive differences in vocation. Bodies of older people, writes Mercer, "demand primacy of place in determining everyday realities and are often experienced as limiting factors." Bodies and movement slow down as we age. The healing of injuries takes longer, and we move more slowly through life. Younger people find this slowness to be frustrating, counter to the multitasking of their busy lives. Mercer writes:

> It can be hard to see vocation in the slowness. Visiting an older adult with dementia may involve me simply sitting with (or pacing with) that person over a generous expanse of time in which linguistic communication is completely absent. The only thing that "happens" (if such a word even fits) is time shared in the presence of God and one another. Such times may or may not be contemplative, but they will surely be formative of the one who inhabits this slow time with the older adult.[24]

In her list of universal spiritual needs of all people, Lori Amdam, a clinical nurse educator, includes purpose and meaning in life and the "ability to contribute, give back, be grateful." We don't often associate these facets of spirituality with people who have dementia. Amdam believes that caregivers—professionals, family members, or friends—need to find ways that people with dementia can help others. This gives them peace of mind even in circumstances that are not peaceful. Listening is a gift that validates another person. Allowing a person to say aloud his or her concerns, even if the listener has nothing to add, can provide that validation. This is one place where people with dementia can make a contribution.[25]

Time changes when we are with older people, writes Mercer, if we are open to their gifts of listening and being. The narratives that usually drive us, such as family and work, frame time in terms of organization, a constant juggling of events and places. Technologies and devices that help us save time are highly valued. But time spent with older adults, she says, stops being a good to be spent or saved, and instead becomes a sacred space where relationships are created.

> When I visit older adults, I experience the gift of time. It so profoundly reshapes my life that I have come to think of the vocation of older adults (especially those with Alzheimer's and other forms of dementia) as offering time-gifts to people who need to slow down. In this way, the callings of the ones receiving care are inextricably linked to the callings of the ones giving care. . . . receiving [care] becomes the more visible element in daily life, but where giving takes place in unobserved ways.[26]

Looking for and finding God's call, even among the frailest or most disabled among us, gives us a new understanding of human usefulness and value. God's purposes for these people may not be tied to actual work or activity, but to their ability to call forth loyalty, commitment, justice, and even love. They also remind us of our instinctual need for interdependence. "God's call for older adults to receive care from others is also a call to experience the care and presence of God," writes Mercer.[27]

Maria Wellisch recently said that spending time with people who have dementia fortifies her spirit. When the administrative aspects of her work at a large retirement community, especially the numbing rules, sapped her energy, she quietly "escaped" to the memory unit, where she slowed down and found a deep contentment. She felt the beating of her heart slow and her breathing deepen to match the unhurried pace of the people there. Together they experienced the care and presence of God.[28]

Advocacy

The 2017 report from the World Health Organization urged countries and international partners to work to increase awareness of dementia, establish dementia-friendly initiatives, accelerate research and innovation, and increase support for caregivers. The Church as an international body has the potential to have significant impact on the problem by joining in these efforts.

The Church of England was one of the pioneers in establishing the "Dementia-Friendly Church" movement. The Lichfield Diocese partnered with Livability (a national Christian disability and community engagement charity) to develop ways to make church dementia-friendly.[29] Their practical guide, *Developing a Dementia-Friendly Church*, is published in conjunction with England's Alzheimer's Society.[30] Clergy training is a key feature in England's efforts.

Dementia Friendly America (DFA),[31] an advocacy group based on similar organizations in England, is a network of businesses, care homes, civic organizations, governmental agencies, hospitals, churches, and others that share a particular concern for people with dementia. "ACT on Alzheimer's" and thirty-four dementia-friendly communities in Minnesota worked together to create the group, which was kicked off by the Obama administration in 2015. Its goal is to improve quality of life for people with dementia, to help them to age in place, and to support caregivers who are often unpaid. The underserved, such as people in rural, Latino, and urban African American neighborhoods, are of particular interest. Senator Bill Frist, a national spokesperson for the organization, said, "We're building a nationwide effort to educate Americans about dementia, equip business owners and first responders to recognize and assist those with memory loss, and empower people with Alzheimer's and dementia to engage independently and safely in community life for as long as possible."[32] Congregations can get involved through their local chapter. Many resources are also available through the Alzheimer's Association and USAgainstAlzheimer's (the latter includes the multifaith USClergyAgainstAlzheimer's.)

Embracing Our Mission

For too long we have assumed that caring for people with dementia is a one-way street. As the cognitive skills and comprehension of those with dementia decrease over time, we have been so caught up in their losses that we fail to see the many qualities that remain. While diseases like Alzheimer's cause degeneration of brain cells, many functions of the brain continue. A love for chocolate or ice cream can last as long as the body can process it. A sense of humor can outlast the loss of memory if we simply look for it. Christine Bryden reminds us that the self that has defined a person throughout life never disappears. The deep love between a mother and daughter remains even when the mother no longer remembers her daughter's name. Anne Karoly reflected on her mother's love that surfaced at unexpected times:

> Sometimes, sitting in her chair, she beckons me to lean in until our noses touch. "You will never know how much I love you," she says. Hugging back, I tell her, "You are my best mom."[33]

Dementia takes us down difficult roads that don't always end with laughter or hugs or even in peace. The need for constant care of people affected not only by brain disease, but also by the changing needs of an aging body, often leaves us exhausted and empty. And our unspoken fears take a toll. Jade Angelica learned from her mother who had Alzheimer's how to overcome her fear of dementia, which allowed her to embrace their relationship fully.

> I see that [people living with dementia] still have the potential to inspire us, teach us, love us, heal us, amuse us, befriend us, calm us, touch us,

energize us, enlighten us, empower us, forgive us, nurture us, open our hearts, bring out the best in us, and bring meaning and purpose into our lives. We may be surprised to realize that persons with Alzheimer's still have the capacity to show us how to be humble and trusting and courageous and receptive; how to be authentically ourselves in this present moment; how to be guileless, innocent and completely without sin.[34]

By understanding and embracing the redemptive qualities of dementia, we can begin to see God's redeeming power in our own lives. We see this more clearly when we are accompanied by caring people in our faith communities, new friends discovered at Memory Cafés, and others with personal and professional understanding of dementia. Our journey leads us beyond science, beyond theology, beyond the intellect, beyond even memory to the heart, understanding fully that "neither death, nor life, nor angels, nor rulers, nor things present, nor things to come, nor powers, nor height, nor depth, nor anything else in all creation, will be able to separate us from the love of God in Christ Jesus our Lord" (Romans 8:38–39).

Reflection Questions

* How could your congregation welcome people with dementia fully into its community life? How could they be integrated into areas of service, such as greeting, ushering, and layreading?

* Could your congregation partner with other faith communities to offer special worship services or Memory Cafés for your community?

* How could your community tap into the gifts of people who have dementia? How can your faith community discover those gifts?

* What steps could your faith community take to advocate for the diverse needs of people with dementia?

Notes

1. Christine Bryden and Elizabeth MacKinlay, "Dementia—a Spiritual Journey Towards the Divine: A Personal View of Dementia," in *Mental Health and Spirituality in Later Life*, ed. Elizabeth MacKinlay (New York: Haworth Pastoral Press, 2002), 73.
2. Christine Bryden, "A Continuing Sense of Self Within the Lived Experience of Dementia," presentation at the Seventh International Conference on Ageing

and Spirituality, June 4-7, 2017, Chicago, Illinois, accessed June 16, 2017, www.7thinternationalconference.org.

3. Anne Karoly, "Dementia Has Destroyed My Mother's Memory, but Not Her Surety of God's Presence," *Faith & Leadership,* June 27, 2017, accessed March 16, 2018, https://www.faithandleadership.com/anne-karoly-dementia-has-destroyed -my-mothers-memory-not-her-surety-gods-presence.

4. Audrey Scanlan and Linda Snyder, *Rhythms of Grace: Worship and Faith Formation for Children and Families with Special Needs* (Denver: Morehouse Education Resources, 2010), 5-18.

5. Bryden, "A Continuing Sense of Self."

6. James W. Farwell, interview by Dorothy Linthicum, October 30, 2017 at Virginia Theological Seminary, Alexandria, Virginia.

7. The Book of Common Prayer (New York: The Church Hymnal Corporation, 1979), 400.

8. Farwell interview.

9. James W. Farwell, *The Liturgy Explained* (Harrisburg, PA: Morehouse Publishing, 2013), 17-18, 38-44.

10. Marjorie Thompson, *Soul Feast: An Invitation to the Christian Spiritual Life* (Louisville, KY: Westminster John Knox Press, 1995), cited in Sara Robb and Greg Smith, "Church at Home: Small-Group Worship for Isolated Elders," presentation at the Seventh International Conference on Ageing and Spirituality, June 4-7, 2017, Chicago, Illinois, accessed June 16, 2017, https://www .7thinternationalconference.org/copy-of-plenary-speakers.

11. Robb and Smith, "Church at Home."

12. Ibid.

13. Audrey Scanlan, "Transformative Formation Opens Minds and Hearts," *Episcopal Teacher* 30, no. 2 (2018): 15, accessed March 1, 2018, https://vts .myschoolapp.com/ftpimages/95/download/download_2642490.pdf.

14. Bère Miesen, "Care-giving in Dementia: Contours of a Curriculum," *Dementia: The International Journal of Social Research and Practice* 9, no. 4 (2010): 473-489, doi:10.1177/1471301210381680.

15. Sally Quinn, "He was Behaving Differently. He had Lost Something. I was the Only One Who Noticed," *Washington Post*, September 6, 2017, C-1.

16. Memory Café Guidelines: Jytte Fogh Lokvig, "The Alzheimer's and Memory Café: How to Start and Succeed with Your Own Café" (Santé Fe: Endless Circle Press, 2016); "The Massachusetts Memory Café Toolkit" (2016), accessed December 18, 2017, http://www.jfcsboston.org/Portals/0/Uploads/Documents /Memory%20Caf%C3%A9%20Toolkit/Massachusetts%20Memory%20 Caf%C3%A9%20Toolkit.pdf; "The Neighborhood Memory Café Tool Kit" (2012), accessed December 18, 2018, http://www.thirdageservices.com/Memory %20Cafe%20Tool%20Kit.pdf.

17. Community of Hope International (COH) website, http://www.cohinternational .org.
18. Ibid.
19. Maria L. Wellisch, "A Hope for Community becomes a Community of Hope," presented at the Abundant Living 14th Annual Conference, March 6-8, 2017, Camp Allen, Diocese of Texas.
20. Ibid.
21. COH website.
22. Helen Appelberg on the COH website.
23. Joyce Ann Mercer, "What Does Christian Vocation Look Like for the Elderly?" *The Christian Century*, June 23, 2017, accessed December 20, 2017, https://www .christiancentury.org/article/features/what-does-christian-vocation-look -elderly.
24. Ibid.
25. Lori Amdam, "Spiritual Care for People with Dementia: Practical Tips," Tapestry Foundation for Health Care (presentation September 24, 2012, Vancouver, British Columbia, Canada), accessed December 8, 2017, https://www.youtube. com/watch?v=ccRx5wRrEBo.
26. Mercer, "Christian Vocation."
27. Ibid.
28. Maria Wellisch, telephone interview by Dorothy Linthicum, December 15, 2017.
29. Robert Friedrich and Robert Woods, "Developing Dementia-Friendly Churches," *Journal of Dementia Care* 24, no. 5 (2016): 18-20.
30. *Developing a Dementia-Friendly Church: A Practical Guide,* accessed January 2, 2018, https://cofehereford.contentfiles.net/media/assets/file/Dementia-Friendly -Church-Guide.pdf.
31. Dementia Friendly America, http://www.dfamerica.org.
32. "Dementia Friendly America Initiative Launches in Communities Across the U.S., from Maryland to California," USAgainstAlzheimer's, accessed December 18, 2017, https://www.usagainstalzheimers.org/press/dementia-friendly-america -initiative-launches-communities-across-us-maryland-california.
33. Karoly, "My Mother's Memory."
34. Jade Angelica, "Seeing the True Value of Our Loved Ones with Alzheimer's When Our Vision Is Blurred by Tears," *Huffington Post*, March 30, 2015, accessed January 2, 2018, https://www.huffingtonpost.com/jade-c-angelica/ alzheimers-dementia-value_b_6563906.html.

Finding God in the Midst of Dementia

Living with dementia often means going back, retracing steps, finding lost items. Robert Atchley notes, "Many people with advanced dementia may not be able to tell you much about who or where they are or who the people around them are, but they still exhibit many of the traits we prize most in personhood—kindness toward others, listening to the life stories of others, and caring for one another."[1]

In his book *Spirituality and Aging*, Atchley identified three basic forms of spirituality as an intense awareness of the present, transcendence of the personal self, and a feeling of connection with all of life, the universe, a supreme being, or a great web of being.[2] Isn't it ironic that people who have dementia, the very condition we fear, can so easily enter one or more of these forms of spirituality?

Awareness of the Present

People with dementia seem to be able to live fully in the present. They call us again and again to the present. They are who they are without apology, living in a world turned upside down, filled with loneliness, uncertainty, and the kindness of strangers. If we slow down and enter their world with them, we may at first feel their anxiety and fear. But if we listen carefully, they can teach us about surviving the unknown, sometimes with grace and dignity or sometimes with stubbornness and spite. Dementia doesn't change who they are, but it can mask their identity from us if we don't look hard enough.

*   *   *

Longing for home is a common theme among those with dementia. I can't know for certain, but I think my mother was constantly searching for the familiar, as much a state of mind as a three-dimensional place. Gliding past a mirror, she would search to see a face she recognized. Looking out a window, she scanned the view for a person, a gait, a place that provided a memory of home.

A few weeks before she died, she had dinner with John, her twenty-one-year-old grandson. They had always had a very playful relationship and were not averse to pranks. During dinner a crumb fell next to her plate. She carefully picked it up and put it next to John's plate. He looked her in the eye, and very intentionally moved it back toward her plate. She sighed and looked away, while easy conversation flowed among us. Without looking down, she inched her hand toward the crumb and pushed it back toward John.

Without missing a beat, he slowly passed it back to her. That's when they both started grinning. Their moods were infectious, and we finished dinner with laughter and companionship. For a few moments at least, mom was home, and all was well.—*Dorothy*

*   *   *

Transcendence of the Personal Self

In the busyness of our lives, those who don't have symptoms of dementia often spend too much time looking back or forward. They depend on linear time, which can be a gift when enduring unpleasant moments. Whatever is happening will eventually end, if they can but endure.

At the same time, linear time too often rules people's thinking and limits their imaginations about who and what and where God is. Surely God moves easily from one dimension to another, all knowing and all powerful. If they can escape to a nonlinear view of time by stepping outside a current reality, they can loosen their ties to preconceived ideas and begin to see a situation or incident more clearly. They have the opportunity to re-evaluate old events to gain new perspectives and perhaps find opportunities to right old wrongs. Those with dementia, the same people that some describe as having lost their humanity, are able to transcend a current state to an alternate reality that makes sense in a world too often filled with confusion. The new place they enter often brings them both comfort and delight.

In chapter 1, we referred to a popular YouTube video showing that long-term memory of music can survive dementia. The video also illustrates how music can help people from all walks of life transcend a current reality to an alternate dimension of joy and love.[3] The video features Henry, who had been mostly silent for many years. Music opens his memories, and he begins to talk about the power of love in the world. A world fashioned by love is, perhaps, closer to the reality of God's Kingdom than the reality of the silent place where Henry had been living for so many years. Perhaps by going with others into an alternate reality, we may find ourselves on holy ground.

Connection with All of Life

People with dementia seem to connect with the universe and God with such ease, less interested in questions and doubts that may have filled their minds in the past. In describing her mother's relationship with God, Anne Karoly wrote:

> I have taken care of mom for six years. I have watched as her memories and abilities disappear. But I marvel at what remains: Her surety of God's presence in her life. . . . She is not a burden. I mean it. It is an honor to have a front row seat to her dementia and her stalwart faith. . . . I ask her why we are attending church. Mom says, "To talk with Jesus and to share our love." She may have forgotten how to dress herself, but she has not forgotten this.[4]

Universal Spiritual Needs

Connections among people matter for their spiritual well-being, says clinical nurse Lori Amdam. She identifies six universal spiritual needs for all people, not just those with dementia. Those needs are:

1. To have purpose and meaning in life
2. To connect to others: to have respect and be appreciated; to belong; and to be known
3. To love and be loved
4. To be hopeful, have comfort and peace of mind
5. To contribute, give back and be grateful
6. To forgive and be reconciled[5]

When these needs are met, spiritual well-being is met, Amdam says. "When you hear people call out over and over, 'Help me!' or 'When can I go home?' or you see people looking to escape, we know that is a manifestation of spiritual distress."[6] When we treat spirituality as a resource, it can become a strength and provide hope. Amdam believes caregivers can tap into a person's spirituality by identifying those who provided strength and hope in the past and by returning to practices in the past that helped the person cope with illness, pain, or loss.

Earlier in chapter 5 we cited Richard Rohr's description of the two tasks of life: to first build a "container" or identity, and second to "find the contents that the container was meant to hold."[7] Rohr emphasizes the importance of establishing identity and a more cohesive self, but never mentions the need for rationality to complete life tasks.

After spending time with people at different stages of dementia, we feel that the disease does not necessarily diminish wisdom that comes from experience. Those with dementia may eventually not be able to express their wisdom verbally, but they may show it in other ways interspersed with moments of verbal lucidity. Whether caregivers and others gain the value of this wisdom depends on the time spent with people who have dementia, observing and listening to them. Containers are still being filled and life tasks completed by those with dementia if people take the time to look.

What We Learned

After our journey of discovery in writing this book, where have we arrived and what have we learned? In the preface, we described Dorothy's response to James Goodwin's description of Alzheimer's as a learning disability. How did she heed Robert Atchley's call to find the truth and deal with it? Being together for the journey, both authors were fellow travelers and teachers for each other.

Being more aware of the power of language has helped us be more respectful of people who equate memory loss and dementia with aging. Their fear of brain disease transfers to aging, resulting in an avoidance of this special stage in life that God has ordained. And we are simply more aware of using the word "Alzheimer's." In general, there is still much we don't know about the diseases that cause dementia. Why does the same plaque that is thought to destroy neurons appear in some people who don't show the symptoms of Alzheimer's? Why does this disease affect life expectancy so differently among people diagnosed with it? We don't avoid reality or the suffering caused by diseases associated with dementia, but we do backpedal from making our own diagnosis or speaking from knowledge we don't possess.

Our minds are more open to other options about memory loss and the symptoms of dementia. Some memory loss is a part of aging for most people. Mental file drawers of people over seventy are filled to overflowing. Because they cannot find that elusive word or name they haven't used in a while doesn't mean much. If they drop the search, that name or word often pops up later after their subconscious unearths it. The same rationale goes for lost keys. Most people have been misplacing keys since they started carrying them. But now they blame age, rather than a lack of focus when they laid them down. In the past year, we've become less hard on others and ourselves in our expectations.

We are becoming better listeners. We try to listen with our hearts as well as our minds. We try to filter out our own experiences with dementia, which are tied up in emotions and memories that are flawed and filled with regret, guilt, anger, and relief. When we feel emotions creeping into our reactions to someone's story, we note them and set them aside to work through later.

James Goodwin was wrong—and right: dementia is not a learning disability, but by demonizing dementia, we diminish those who have it. As we think and talk about people who have memory loss, we discover similarities and commonalities with disabilities in general. John Swinton notes that "People with profound intellectual disabilities and people with dementia are in the same situation—they are objects of other people's projection. . . . We project loss onto these people." He asks, "What does it mean to be fully human and at the same time have a profound disability?" Swinton (like Goodwin) includes people with dementia as part of a generic grouping of people with disabilities.[8] Swinton says:

The problem for people with disabilities or dementia is that the first thing you think is that these people don't have reason, that they're dependent and they need someone to look after them—so they're unworthy, they're not persons. But in reality, we are all only persons in relationships; people with disabilities remind us of who we are.[9]

As we noted in chapter 4, other theologians have made observations about the full participation in our congregations by people with disabilities. Theologians Nancy Eiesland and Don Saliers bring new understandings to the Church about liturgy, interpretation of scripture, and biblical healing rituals for the disabled. Saliers describes a healing service at Saint John's Abbey in south central Minnesota, attended by several elderly monks living in the monastery infirmary. They were seated in an inner circle of chairs that were spaced to accommodate their various disabilities. As the rite of anointing was about to begin, those sitting in an outer circle were invited to come forward and lay hands on those in the center.

As the blessed oils were applied to those hands and those foreheads, the rest of us followed by touching with a simple word of blessing the whole circle of those elders. This took time. A slow adagio dance. A remarkable circle . . . and the tears intermingled with the fragrance of the oil and the rhythm of this luminous dance of blessing.[10]

Eiesland and Saliers ask about the "questions, insights, and perspectives that would be advanced if people with disabilities, in all their diversity, were placed at the center of theological education rather than at the periphery—to which they have too often been relegated."[11] We would be forced to talk *with* rather than *about* people with disabilities, including dementia.

As we noted in chapter 7, some sound sources of materials for planning and adapting liturgy for people with dementia, for example, come from resources created for children on the autism spectrum. We recognize the vast differences between older people with dementia and children who are just beginning their life journeys. However, they share similar liturgical needs for shorter services, clear language, simple sentences, and the freedom to move around. Music is vital for both groups, but selections need to be tailored to their traditions and preferences.

At the same time, we don't want to trivialize other dementia-related issues, such as loss of logic, poor health, and personality changes that move beyond memory loss and disability. These changes take additional tolls on caregivers and add confusion to those in the early stages of dementia as well as those in later phases.

We are discovering that what we learned while working with children, youth, and young adults is applicable to ministry with older adults. Older people often tell us they don't want to be treated "differently." Maybe we should work a little harder to cross the age lines—not by turning exclusively to intergenerational programming, but by applying what we learn from one age group to another. The Godly Play curriculum, used primarily with children, is now used with adults at several levels. In *Graceful Nurture: Using Godly Play with Adults*, Rebecca McClain describes creative courses for adults that are adapted from key Godly Play lessons. Storytellers across the country who work with frail elders and those with dementia use Godly Play stories because the "artifacts," storytelling props of characters and settings, help listeners stay connected to stories even if their minds wander.[12]

Jerome Berryman, the creator of Godly Play®, has studied the spirituality of childhood for many years and believes those of us in churches are too reliant on vocabulary, especially our use of "church" words, such as font, covenant, confession, and theology. He argues that all people have experiences of God and with God, no matter their age or physical state. We are called to respect those experiences even if a person is unable to talk about them or describe them in any way. Since words may not be an avenue to understanding someone's experience with God, says Berryman, maybe we need to watch, and listen, and be with that person, learning to know what he or she knows.[13]

When we set aside our fears, it is easier to find Christ in each person around us. When Dorothy was a young mother, she began volunteering one day a week at one of Mother Teresa's houses for men who had AIDs. The nuns who ran the house were both ordinary and extraordinary. They chose to live simple lives serving and praising God from the time they got up until they went to bed. They accepted everyone who entered their house with the expectation that they would find Christ in each visitor, whether they came to mop floors and wash clothes, or were terribly ill.

By allowing our expectations to be formed by prayer, we can begin to see Christ within people who have dementia. By finding Christ in others, we begin to discover the Christ in us.

* * *

For much of the time my dad lived on the closed wing of his retirement community, he thought he was at a church recreation center, similar to a facility in his Baptist church in Oklahoma. He was amazed by the kindness of the people who helped him and their willingness to share their food at every meal. I was grateful to the staff of this Methodist home, especially the immigrant caregivers who looked after him with grace and respect.

The home was close to my office, so I could visit regularly at different times of the day. I often arrived with an agenda. Today I would cut his hair, or do his nails, or go outside for a stroll. But he finally taught me that the best visits had no agenda.

When I came into his presence, his face lit up with a big smile. He wasn't sure who I was—he vaguely thought I might be his wife—but he knew that he loved me and that I loved him. On those do-nothing days we mostly would sit together. After a brief splutter of conversation, we sat in silence. Dad would occasionally nod off, only to awaken with that same radiant smile he had first greeted me with. My thoughts stopped churning after a while as I came completely into the present with him.

After he died, I realized how much I missed those silent moments together, marked with a richness that I have rarely recaptured. I can still see his smile in my mind's eye as I realize I am smiling too.—*Dorothy*

* * *

Where is God when we are afraid? In working with adolescents, the truth youth leaders emphasize over and over is that the young people are never alone. Perhaps this message needs to be the clarion call for people as they grow older and are faced with a myriad of problems and maybe even dementia. We are never alone. God is always with us, even when we cannot feel or even talk about God's presence. Paul writes in Romans 8:38–39, "For I am convinced that neither death, nor life, nor angels, nor rulers, nor things present, nor things to come, nor powers, nor height, nor depth, nor anything else in all creation, will be able to separate us from the love of God in Christ Jesus our Lord."

Instead of focusing on lost memories and losing the control that most have sought since they were toddlers, it is time to concentrate on hope. Each person is still God's creation, no matter their age, and they are good. That love that Paul describes isn't directed at the people they once were; it comes from a God who loves them for the people they are now.

Redeeming Our Lives

Recently a student at Virginia Theological Seminary preached on John 12:24: "Very truly, I tell you, unless a grain of wheat falls into the earth and dies it remains just a single grain; but if it dies, it bears much fruit." She noted that many listening to her speak had experienced transitions of some kind. "We have all buried things in the ground along the way so that a single grain might bear much fruit. It is part of our reality of resurrection. Death and life are experienced not only in the biggest and most definite terms, but in the little daily moments when we give something up or let something die to make room for God's grace to live and grow in our lives."[14]

Those with dementia often don't have control over where they live, when they have to get up, what they eat, or who they can see. They have had to bury parts of their lives they no longer control nor can remember. And yet they invite us to join them in the present, to dance with them in an alternative reality that transcends our worlds, and to connect intimately with God. They ask us to put negative opinions, judgments, expectations, or goals into the ground so everyone can live in the places they find themselves now. Finally, they ask us to embrace the hope of the resurrection. In doing so, God can redeem dementia for all of us.

Notes

1. Robert Atchley, *Spirituality and Aging* (Baltimore: The Johns Hopkins University Press, 2009), 42.
2. Ibid., 2.

3. "Man in Nursing Home reacts to Hearing Music from His Era," YouTube, musicandmemory.org. https://www.youtube.com/watch?v=fyZQf0p73QM (accessed November 6, 2017).

4. Anne Karoly, "Dementia Has Destroyed My Mother's Memory, but Not Her Surety of God's Presence," *Faith & Leadership*, June 27, 2017, accessed March 16, 2018, https://www.faithandleadership.com/anne-karoly-dementia-has-destroyed -my-mothers-memory-not-her-surety-gods-presence.

5. Lori Amdam, "Spiritual Care for People with Dementia: Practical Tips," Tapestry Foundation for Health Care (presentation September 24, 2012, Vancouver, British Columbia, Canada), accessed December 8, 2017, https://www.youtube .com/watch?v=ccRx5wRrEBo.

6. Ibid.

7. Richard Rohr, *Falling Upward* (New York: Jossey-Bass, 2011), xiii.

8. Chelsea Temple Jones, "Interview with John Swinton," *UC Observer,* February 2013, accessed November 14, 2017 http://www.ucobserver.org/ interviews/2013/02/john_swinton.

9. Ibid.

10. Don E. Saliers, "Toward a Spirituality of Inclusiveness," in *Human Disability and the Service of God: Reassessing Religious Practice,* ed. Nancy L. Eiesland and Don E. Saliers (Nashville: Abington Press, 1998), 19-20.

11. Nancy L. Eiesland and Don E. Saliers, eds., *Human Disability and the Service of God: Reassessing Religious Practice* (Nashville: Abington Press, 1998), 16.

12. Rebecca McClain, *Graceful Nurture: Using Godly Play with Adults* (New York: Church Publishing, 2017).

13. Jerome Berryman, *Godly Play: An Imaginative Approach to Religious Education.* (Minneapolis: Augsburg Fortress, 1995).

14. Samantha Gottlich Smith, "Bury it in the Dirt. Let it Die," senior sermon preached at Immanuel Chapel, Virginia Theological Seminary, September 9, 2016.

Further Reading

Print

Kathy Berry. *When Words Fail: Practical Ministry to People with Dementia and Their Caregivers*. Centennial, CO: FaithHappening Publishers, 2016.

Websites

Spirituality and Dementia: http://www.spiritualityanddementia.org

Older Adult Ministry Resources (Virginia Theological Seminary):
https://www.vts.edu/page/center-for-the-ministry-of-teaching/older-adult
 -ministry-resources

Free online booklets from Methodist Homes (MHA) in England:
Growing Dementia-Friendly Churches
https://www.mha.org.uk/files/6013/8900/8979/Spiritual_Care_and_
 People_with_Dementia_2011.pdf
Spiritual Care and People with Dementia: a Basic Guide
https://www.mha.org.uk/files/6013/8900/8979/Spiritual_Care_and_People
 _with_Dementia_2011.pdf
Worship and People with Dementia
https://www.mha.org.uk/files/2314/1105/5961/17578_Dementia_Worship
 _NEW_2014_v2_12.09.pdf
Visiting People with Dementia
https://www.mha.org.uk/files/9914/1105/5872/17578_Dementia_Visiting
 _NEW_2014_v4_12.09.pdf